BRITISH FOREIGN POLICY AND
THE ATLANTIC AREA

BRITISH FOREIGN POLICY AND THE ATLANTIC AREA

The Techniques of Accommodation

Arthur Cyr

HOLMES & MEIER PUBLISHERS, INC.
New York

First published in the United States of America 1979 by
HOLMES & MEIER PUBLISHERS, INC.
30 Irving Place, New York, N.Y. 10003

Library of Congress Cataloging in Publication Data

Cyr, Arthur I   1945–
    British foreign policy and the Atlantic area.

    Bibliography: p.
    Includes index.
    1. Great Britain—Foreign relations—1945-
2. North Atlantic region—Politics and government.
I. Title.
DA588.C93   1979   327.41   79–4331
ISBN 0-8419-0489-8

PRINTED IN GREAT BRITAIN

Contents

List of Tables

Introduction

The purpose of this book is to provide a general overview and analysis of British foreign policy in the period since the close of the Second World War. Particular attention is given to relationships within the Atlantic area, the region of most consequence to postwar British foreign policy. As that nation has retreated from broadly based international empire and influence, there has been more direct and explicit engagement in European affairs, principally through membership of the European Community. Entry into the Community, finally achieved on 1 January 1973 after two earlier rebuffs by the French, capped a decade of effort to gain admission and also a much longer period during which the British had been trying to come to terms with the necessity of a new attitude toward Europe. Also in the Atlantic area, the postwar period brought increasing reliance and emphasis upon ties with the United States. That relationship—always special—became clearly more crucial to Britain.

Consequently, attention is particularly focused on relationships with the United States on the one hand and Western Europe on the other. In both cases, there is an effort to place more recent developments in the broader context of the history of relations among the nations involved. The special relationship with the United States has been referred to frequently by both British and American leaders, especially in earlier years of co-operation in crisis during the Second World War and before the decline of Britain became so pronounced. Rarely defined in any explicit sense, it is nevertheless true that the foreign policies of the two nations have been linked by cultural similarities along with the comparatively specific interest in preventing European powers from achieving positions of strong influence within the Americas. British–European relations provide more dramatic evidence of change in British policy in response to diminution of British power. As described more fully later, the decision by Prime Minister Macmillan in 1961 to apply for admission to the European

Community itself capped a period of extensive, if slow-moving, change in British perceptions and policy. In the past, the Continent had been viewed as an area which was important but separate from Britain, an area which could be influenced most successfully if kept at a distance. In characteristic fashion, this most important shift in the national policy to acceptance of formal membership in comprehensive European economic institutions was handled gradually, not abruptly, through a process of coalition-changing and consensus-building within the government and administrative bureaucracy of the nation and the hierarchy of the ruling Conservative Party. The emphasis on gradualism, incrementalism and a consensual approach is developed at length in the study which follows. In addition to concentration on major allies, detailed attention is paid to the structures of decision-making, characteristics of decision-makers and foreign policy professionals, and the broader institutional and cultural environment of the political system.

This book is not designed as an extensive original research effort. There were some interviews with British politicians and civil servants, but main reliance was placed on sources already available. Two different sorts of motives underlay and provided the main motivation for this project. First, during two years of teaching a course on international relations in the Atlantic area, I was impressed by the absence of a reasonably current book on British foreign policy suitable for use as a supplementary text for undergraduate as well as graduate instruction. For this reason, the book which follows is geared as much to the student as to the professional audience.

Second, I have for some time been interested in employing existing literature to attempt to construct a comparatively positive evaluation of the record of British foreign policy during the period since the Second World War. Although there is a fairly clearly indentifiable tradition in the disciplines of political science and history in the United States of examining British political structures and political history with considerable sympathy, in more recent decades the international decline of Britian has been reflected in a more critical and unflattering attitude toward policies and institutions of that nation. British foreign policy, along with domestic politics, has been attacked for drift in face of and sluggishness in adjusting to new circumstances, lack of innovation and imagination, absence of foresight and related shortcomings. The two-party system, which was once praised for encouraging compromise, continuity and stability, has more recently been described as hampering fresh approaches to policy and fresh faces in leadership positions. The current tendency is discussed in this study, which attempts to interpret decisions and events in a manner to give a more equal balance of credit as well as blame to British leadership for the method of the national response to a markedly changed international environment. Related to this, there is development of the basic point that current British political culture, institutions and practices do not reflect an historical departure. The method of gradualism preferred today is in tune with the British approach to great power status in the past. As in the past, there is the virtue of stability and balance to this approach.

Various institutions and individuals assisted in the production of this volume. They are too numerous to cite individually, but some in particular should be mentioned. The Academic Senate of the University of California supported research travel to Britain. Helpful comments and other assistance has been provided by Professors Vincent Davis of the University of Kentucky, Peter Merkl of the University of California at Santa Barbara, and Roman Kolkowicz and Richard Sisson of the University of California at Los Angeles. A revised version of the chapter on British defence policy appeared as a working paper of the UCLA Center for Arms Control and International Security. In different ways, the scholarly resources of that centre were useful in this work. I am sorry indeed that it is not possible to mention by name all the professionals in government in Britain who shared their insights, information and good will. Outside of the civil and diplomatic services, David Astor, Samuel Brittan, Lord Gore-Booth, Stephen Haseler, Thomas McNally and Sir Con O'Neill are among a number of individuals who have been especially helpful to this study.

Arthur Cyr

Chicago, Illinois
August 1978

1 The British Role

INTRODUCTION

This book is an effort to describe and analyse Britain's changing international position since the Second World War, especially in the Atlantic region. Inevitably, it is a chronicle of decline. Reflecting the diminution of power which has occurred, it has been customary in a great deal of academic as well as more popular literature to criticise strongly the nation's specific foreign policies and general approach to international affairs during this period. By contrast, a central thesis of the study which follows is that such attitudes should be balanced by more positive and optimistic considerations. British foreign policy over the last three decades has contained serious blunders and errors of judgement. At the same time, there have been equally striking examples of foresight, sensible flexibility, moderation and shrewd calculation. Viewed most generally, Britain's decline has been an inevitable result of economic, geographical and military factors largely beyond her control. Faced with a dramatic reduction in power and influence, British leadership has adjusted to the new situation with a minimum of trauma and strain.

Britain's future decline was not readily apparent at the conclusion of the Second World War. Britian was then recognised as one of the three leading Allied powers. The series of well-publicised personal conferences involving Churchill, Roosevelt and Stalin highlighted and symbolised this status. Moreover, the British had played a particularly dramatic role during the conflict. In the earlier part of the war, Britain was the besieged island fortress, fighting on alone during the grim months between the fall of France and the entry of the Soviet Union against the Axis. Later, Britain continued to occupy a pivotal position as forward base for Allied bombers, for massing Allied troops, and for launching the invasion of France.

This prominence and importance during the war capped a long

history of very significant British influence in international affairs. Though a small island nation, Britain had nevertheless established an enormous colonial empire and had also conducted a skilful and generally successful diplomacy within Europe. The British approach to European affairs had been dispassionate and independent, with consistent attention to protection of British security by preventing a single Continental power from achieving a dominant position. Given this influential history, it was easy to assume during the Second World War that Britain would continue to enjoy a significant role after the war.

Various factors, international and domestic, have led to the dramatic shift in Britain's position. With the development of the Cold War after the Second World War, Britain was overshadowed by her much more powerful wartime partners. Moreover, the bipolar conflict between the two nuclear giants, the US and the Soviet Union, removed fluidity from the European arena. The division of Germany into two states was reflected in the more general division of Europe, with each half drawn into the orbit of its respective superpower. Consequently, the structure of the new international system prevented Britain from engaging in the sort of balancing among great powers which was its customary historical role. Moreover, while Britain has attempted to operate on several levels of international affairs since 1945, major emphasis has been placed on close relations with the United States. Therefore, the potential advantages of formal and informal consultation have been put above those of independence from the U.S. The British approach has generally been the reverse of the abrasiveness and independence toward the Americans characteristic of France under de Gaulle. The cautious efforts which have been made to further East–West accommodation have lacked the drama or striking success of West Germany's recent initiatives.[1]

The chronic weakness of the British economy has been a major impediment to an assertive stance internationally. Since the end of the Second World War, Britain has been restricted by and preoccupied with problems of slow growth and high unemployment, balance-of-payments deficits, aged and declining industries, severe industrial unrest, and exceptionally high and growing rates of inflation. There has been no British economic miracle comparable to those of Germany or Japan. On the contrary, the nation has slipped from being one of the richest industrial nations to one of the poorest, currently competing with Italy for the position of the weakest economy in the European Economic Community (EEC).

The eclipse of Britain since the war has spurred a variety of criticisms of her definition and conduct of foreign policy. Dean Acheson's often-quoted remark that the British have lost an empire and failed to find a role has been repeated with more detailed arguments of support in a range of scholarly studies. One of the most frequently made points is that British governments have been unwilling to accept consciously the reduced circumstances of the nation, and to plan accordingly. Rather than working within new restrictions, it is alleged, policy-makers have struggled against them. Britain has attempted to maintain a global presence, operating on three separate demanding planes of international relations: the "special relationship" with the United States, and the associated effort to deal on a basis of equality with both superpowers; Europe, first outside and later within the framework of the European Economic Community; and with the rest of the diverse, complex international system through the British Empire and Commonwealth. Henry Kissinger, for example, has written, ". . . that Britain never seemed able to decide which option to pursue: close relations with the United States, a new concept of Commonwealth or an unreserved entry into Europe. By trying to combine all three, Britain ran the risk of losing each."[2]

Often, British efforts to maintain equality with the United States and the Soviet Union, along with wide-ranging international involvements, are viewed as two errors in judgement which reflect a third—British unwillingness to join Europe early, without qualification, as the appropriate arena for concentration of foreign policy attention and energy. Britain has been heavily involved in European affairs, particularly concerning military and security agreements, but has been extremely reluctant to limit or restrict her political independence in pursuit of stronger European community. Kenneth Waltz has noted this ambivalence in describing the British attitude toward the European Economic Community: "The hesitations of Britain's European policy over more than a decade reflected an unwillingness to place Europe above her other interests or even on the same level with them."[3]

Britain's stance toward Europe, while ambiguous on its own terms, is clearly in line with her historic approach to international affairs. The nation's significant influence in the past was linked to a strong tradition of psychological separation from Europe. Her advantage was a function of astute independence, a capacity to get maximum leverage out of economic and military resources through a flexible willingness to shift and move among alliance partners. Britain at its height was an exceptionally powerful nation, but there were other great powers in Europe. The nation's pivotal role was a reflection of its diplomatic skill, which in turn required that physical separation from the Continent be complemented by an attitude of independence. Towards the end of the nineteenth century, Britain entered long-term commitments with Continental states. This shift, however, was dictated by changing domestic and international conditions rather than by an inherent desire for greater co-operation with Europe.[4]

The decline in Britain's international position has also encouraged criticism concerning domestic political institutions and practices. This has occurred on a scholarly as well as a popular level. There is a strong tradition in Anglo-American political science of viewing British government and politics as superior to others. It was particularly common to evaluate the British system in a positive manner during the nineteenth and early twentieth centuries, when the nation was at the height of its power. Walter Bagehot, A. Lawrence Lowell, and Woodrow Wilson are three of the most prominent writers from an earlier age who praised Britain's government. Scholars usually compared the unity of the parliamentary structure favourably with the division and competition characteristic of government in the U.S: the clarity of conflict between the two major parties was contrasted with the confusing mix of party alignments in France.[5]

In recent years, however, there has been an understandable tendency to stress shortcomings of British politics and society, and see new advantages in the American system. Scholars have emphasised the lack of circulation among party and government elites, and recruitment problems resulting from class discrimination in the educational system and society generally. British public policy has been criticised for lack of change and innovation. To a degree, this general problem may be related to the closed, narrow and collegial character of decision-making within British government. The American system, in contrast, may be more difficult to manage, with a much larger and more diverse series of barriers to be hurdled before successful policy development and implementation. At the same time, the system guarantees that a range of viewpoints and opinions are given a hearing. The American requirement that consensus be built laboriously at the national level within the various committees of Congress and the broader administrative sector of government ensures that most major policy innovations are fully discussed; the British capacity to make a number of significant decisions through a rather small group of like-minded people in the Cabinet and highest echelon of the civil service makes it easier to avoid the potential advantages of consulting a large number of varied constituencies.[6]

Much more generally and informally, Britian's reduced global status may be related to a self-critical, caustic tone in a large amount of popular commentary of recent years. Complaints about the directions of foreign policy blend with scathing evaluations of the unhappy "state of Britain". British authors ranging from journalists to playwrights have focused on alleged national self-indulgence, fatigue, unconcern with making the sacrifices required for an important world role, as well as the more clearcut problems associated with the class system and resistance to modernisation in administration of government, industry and other sectors of society. In 1963, the prominent cultural journal *Encounter* devoted an entire issue to elaboration of such themes. While this sort of literature does not provide rigorous data for the social scientist, it does comprise impressionistic commentary for the analyst concerned to understand the domestic context of foreign policy.[7]

In the chapters which follow, concentrated attention is devoted to the impacts and importance of various factors, domestic and international, in the conduct of British foreign policy. There is general examination of economic problems, strategic and military issues, and relationships with the US, Europe and other parts of the globe. Government institutions are discussed, including not only the Foreign Office but other sectors of the bureaucracy. There is also examination of features of the parliamentary and cabinet system, and of the less specific analytical conceptions of political culture and popular attitudes, which impinge upon foreign policy. Continuing attention is given to the interplay of international position and domestic politics.

A major theme is that Britain has handled the transition from global power to middle power with reasonable skill and success. This argument should not be misunderstood. It does not hold that Britain has adjusted as quickly as it might have to a new environment. In fact, a case is developed that Britain would have profited by recognising postwar limitations and restrictions earlier. British leaders tried to operate on a level of rough equality with the United States and the Soviet Union long after this had become impossible. Embarrassments and exertions associated with entering the European Economic Community could have been avoided if the British had decided to join when the organisation was established. The main point of the argument is that Britain's moderate, restrained, flexible approach to international affairs, which served the nation well during its period as a great power, has also enabled it to adjust comparatively easily to markedly reduced status. When a great power, Britain avoided confusing vast influence and an enormous empire with the capacity for creating hegemony or the desirability of doing so. More recently, Britain has moved slowly back from empire and influence without suffering domestic instability, retreat into isolationism, or an erratic foreign policy. The British position has changed, but the moderate style remains.

TRADITIONAL ROLE

The term "balance of power" is used in a variety of senses and contexts by those who study and write about international relations. It may be applied to British foreign policy quite literally, thanks to the continuing national effort to seek security through encouraging competing centres of power on the Continent. It is possible to trace this general approach back to the reign of Henry VIII. In Hans Morgenthau's words, "The classic example of the balance . . . has been provided by Great Britain. To Henry VIII is attributed the maxim: *cui adhaero praeest* (he whom I support will prevail)." According to one applicable story of the time, Henry had a portrait of himself painted in which he held in one hand a pair of scales, labelled respectively Austria and France. In his other hand, he held a weight capable of tipping the balance toward one or the other nation.[8] This image is a useful symbol for British attitudes toward Europe in the centuries which followed. Particular European nations were a source of special concern and danger. Historically, France was a continuing threat. More recently, Germany was the focus of attention. The British approach, however, remained constant even though the tapestry changed. With Europe divided, Britain could feel secure.

Britain employed various specific tools to gain foreign policy ends. The most direct and obvious was military intervention on the side of one nation or the other. While Britain did not have a very large army, its navy was able to provide a powerful complement to the various land forces to which it was coupled by alliance. Additionally, Britain at times used its substantial economic resources to assist one side or another in European conflicts, through providing equipment and supplies or direct money grants and loans. Balance of power politics required alliances, and British economic and naval strength were persuasive incentives for Continental nations.[9]

A necessary corollary of this general British strategy was lack of territorial ambitions within Europe. The nation was neutral in the sense of being in a position to intervene on any side to oppose another which was becoming too powerful. This required that Britain avoid the creation of a continuing coalition of opponents, which in turn dictated restraint of any desires to expand within Europe. As an alternative, the British conquered and colonised large parts of the rest of the globe. It was a game popular with all the great powers of Europe, but the British played it with particular skill and drive. The British Empire provided a number of satisfactions, including formal control over large foreign populations, inexpensive raw materials important to manufacturing industries at home, and the symbolism of power and conquest for use on the European stage.

The flexibility of British policy reflected an approach which was moderate and dispassionate. The British avoided precise theoretical formulations or conscious general policy evaluations. Rather, they were supremely empirical, moving with events rather than trying to anticipate them in detail. The British method was to mitigate and dilute conflict, rather than sharpening and heightening differences; and to search for possible compromise rather than seeking total victory. Britain pursued shifting alliances in order to address changing situations. Policy was therefore reactive, attempting to limit concentrations of power, halt tendencies toward rigidity, and remain alert to development of instability. Among other things, the British were required by these goals to live with inconsistency and to prevent lines of conflict from being drawn too starkly. Waltz has with insight described the style: "To proceed by a sidling movement rather than move directly toward an object, to underplay one's hand, to dampen conflicts and depreciate dangers, to balance parties off against one another, to compromise rather than fight, to postpone decisions, to obscure issues rather than confront them, to move as it were by elision from one position in policy to another. . ."[10]

This tradition retains its strong hold on British foreign policy style, but at the same time the nation's freedom of manoeuvre has been restricted. Since the last part of the nineteenth century, a variety of factors have limited and reduced Britain's old balancing role. The nation's decline since the Second World War has been dramatic, but the roots of it go much farther back in time.

Political changes in Europe began to limit Britain's room for manoeuvre in the closing decades of the last century. Bismarck's skill in creating security for Germany through a variety of competing alliances was not matched by his successors, and the twentieth century began with Europe clearly divided into two *blocs* strongly locked into military competition. After one hundred years of limited and infrequent wars, the First World War brought total war that was extraordinarily devastating. The nations of Europe had not appreciated the impact that technology would have on weapons and strategy, and were unprepared for the length and severity of the war.

During the period after the First World War, Britain remained true to its balancing policy, but without positive effect. European politics had become extremely unstable. The punitive settlement of the war fed German bitterness, which in turn led to support for the uncompromising Hitler regime. The Munich conference was a characteristic British effort to avoid war through accommodation, but only encouraged German ambitions. Growth of ideological politics had implications for the European international system which were not appreciated by Britain, except for Churchill, and he of course was focusing on the menace of Hitler rather than the possibility of a less influential role for Britain.[11]

As noted earlier, the system after the Second World War represents a great departure from the old European structure of international affairs. Changes include the development of bipolarity involving the US and the Soviet Union, and the resulting division of Europe. Beyond that, there was a fundamental shift in the structure of the international system. The earlier system was largely confined to a handful of European states. They were not only roughly equal in power, they were few in number, with cultures and histories which were similar but not identical. As a result, the major nations had a comparability of view concerning the nature of alliances and foreign relations. This in turn facilitated a diplomacy of movement, calculation and limited wars. By contrast, the current system involves not only a confrontation between two nuclear superpowers, but is much larger and replete with various ideological and political divisions. The system is now global rather than European. The two superpowers confront an ideological gulf as well as a competition for power; their domestic political systems and conceptions of future development of human society conflict dramatically. The other states which make up the international system vary greatly in size and power, cultural and historical experiences, and domestic regimes. To some extent, the system has been growing in size and complexity through this century. It was in 1902, for example, that Britain went beyond Europe to form an alliance with Japan as part of the effort to balance and restrain Russian expansion in Asia. The growing economic power of the United States has made it significant to Europe since the last century. Nevertheless, it has been only since the Second World War that the total number of states participating in international relations has expanded dramatically. The size and diversity of the international order not only makes it impossible to pursue easily the flexible British approach, it also calls attention to the decline of the British Empire. Colonies have become independent nations, with Britain currently reduced largely to its own national borders.[12]

In the present international system, it has become common to refer to the United States as having replaced Britain as the dominant power. Considered in detail, the two states actually differ significantly in outlook and approach. Britain at the height of its power was operating in a geographically limited system of states, in which it endeavoured to prevent rigid *blocs* from developing or one nation from becoming exceptionally powerful. The British goal was to lighten national burdens and maintain diversity of power within Europe. The United States, on the other hand, has been anxious to assume significant military obligations through the formation of regional alliances to surround the Communist powers. The goal has been to meet one clearcut *bloc* with another. Britain feared the results of alliance-building among various states; the US has concentrated its anxieties on the Soviet Union, the only state with power sufficient to threaten American survival. While *détente* has recently made the picture more complex, the general American foreign policy approach since the Second World War has been reasonably clearcut. The US has been very sensitive to differences with the Soviet Union, and has acted by directly confronting the challenge represented by the enormous capacity of the other superpower. Whether duelling with the Soviets in crisis, or proposing possible solutions to particular conflicts, the Americans have met them head on rather than through a British combination of ambiguous moves.[13]

From a different perspective, however, it is possible to draw some parallels between the earlier British and current American positions. Both countries have possessed great economic power during their periods of dominance, and willingness to employ it to aid and intimidate others. Both have rightly considered themselves to be of central importance in the international system, with power and influence decisive in character. Both states have had particular military advantages. The American nuclear dominance has only in recent years been challenged by the Soviet Union. In the eighteenth and nineteenth centuries, British naval firepower overshadowed that of other nations. Finally, discussion of the positions of the two in comparable terms has been encouraged by the fact that British decline has taken place approximately in correlation with the rise of the US. Changes in the power of each have been particularly dramatic since the Second World War. After a long history of growing power but isolation from European affairs, the US became heavily involved there and all around the world. After centuries of playing a crucial role in Europe, Britain was unexpectedly unable to continue doing so. Each shift has required an enormous national adjustment. While Britain's current weakness results from developments which can be traced back into the last century, it is only over the past three decades that decline has become apparent.

THE POSTWAR PERIOD

The international system was transformed by the Second World War. The United States and the Soviet Union had suffered heavy casualties, indeed those of the latter had been enormous. Nevertheless, they emerged from the war in dominant positions of power and influence. Two once-powerful states, Germany and Japan, whose foreign adventures had led directly to the war, were largely and quite literally in ruins, their economies shattered and military capabilities destroyed. Europe had generally been devastated by the war, and nations were absorbed with the burdens of rebuilding their economies and domestic political structures overturned by occupation.

Britain was in a more ambiguous position. The war had been costly but had been fought to a successful conclusion. As one of the three principal Allied victors, there was no incentive to reflect on the possibility of a reduced future position. Virtually all the other major nations of Europe had undergone the jarring shocks of military defeat and occupation, destruction of their domestic political orders, and vast social dislocations. This led in turn to a need to begin political life anew after the war, and to plan for a changed international environment. British success in fending off the German military assault meant that more subtle and slow-moving postwar economic threats were neglected.[14]

While it was generally perceived in Britain that international relations were in a state of flux, there was no great uncertainty concerning the position of the nation. British success in the war followed a long history of great international victories and accomplishments. The continuity of history was too firm to encourage doubts. Leon Epstein described the British attitude of the time: "For within the memory of men still living. . .the British were the top dogs of Europe and of the world. Their superiority was of such import and duration that finally, in the recent past, there was no need to boast after the manner of new rivals for world power."[15] Neither of Britain's two major political parties wished to change the nation's course or style in foreign affairs, or contemplate the possibility of greatly reduced status. Even before the conclusion of the war, there had been a general election and change of government in Britain. The Labour Party was victorious in the elections of 1945, with the result that Clement Attlee replaced Churchill as Prime Minister. The change was surprising to many, particularly in the US. Churchill, after all, had led the Coalition government through the harrowing war years. (Actually, one significant difference between British and American politics has been the comparatively greater importance of party label rather than candidate in Britain.) The election returns were not nearly so much a defeat for Churchill personally as for the Conservative Party as a political organisation. The Tories were associated in the popular mind with various national ills and government shortcomings. The party had dominated governments of the 1930s, years of economic depression and hardship. It was also identified with appeasement of Hitler before the war.

The change of government brought ripples rather than reverberations in international affairs. Though the election of Labour brought substantial reforms in domestic areas, primarily in social policy and limited efforts at economic nationalisation, there were no significant foreign policy departures. To a degree, the smooth transition was aided by the fact that the Labour leadership had been involved in the wartime Coalition. Anthony Eden, during the first House of Commons debate after the formation of the new government, made the point that there had never been a serious rift in foreign policy between Conservative and Labour members of the Coalition. The new Foreign Secretary, Ernest Bevin, agreed. This experience had been significantly different from that during the First World War, when a Labour representative did not join the Cabinet until the end of 1916, after a number of basic war policy decisions had been made.[16]

Those minor differences in tone and theme which existed between Tory and Labour were quickly overcome by the demands of the emerging Cold War, which led to increasing dependence on the US and a clear break with the Soviet Union. Bevin, in contrast to

Churchill, was personally hostile to conceptions of geographical spheres of influence and sympathetic to efforts for international stability through the agency of the United Nations. However, East–West conflict was making acceptance of division of Europe unavoidable for the British, and was also frustrating possibilities for harmonious international co-operation through the United Nations.[17]

Though the leaders of the Labour government were anxious to maintain Britain's international influence, they soon found instead that the US was increasingly dominant. It was not only that the Americans were powerful and determined to remain significantly involved in international affairs. Britain was becoming immersed in severe economic problems which had been long in developing and could no longer be ignored. As economic problems increased in severity, the British of necessity constricted their overseas involvements. Since the US was at this time both very powerful and determined to develop further its international leadership, British retreat created vacuums which the Americans rather naturally filled. In Germany, the American and British occupation zones were merged, in part to provide some relief to the latter. The British sector was largely made up of industrial areas. It had never been a significant food producer for the rest of the country. At the same time, the Soviets were proving unco-operative by not allowing food from their eastern zone, which was principally agricultural, to be shipped to the rest of Germany. In consequence, the British had been forced to undertake the large added burden of providing food and other subsidies to their zone.

Comparable patterns of British withdrawal and American advance characterised developments elsewhere. A continuing Communist insurgency had resulted in the presence of British troops in Greece since the end of 1944. The fact that the Greek regime had a dictatorial character led to serious pressures on the Labour government from the party left wing. These were successfully resisted, but it proved nevertheless impossible to sidestep the very different pressures of Britain's worsening economic situation. The government announced that all aid to Greece would cease at the end of March 1947. In addition, Britain was during the same period forced to end assistance to Turkey.[18]

This led directly to one of the most significant and literally far-reaching American policy statements of the postwar period, the Truman Doctrine. It was assumed in Washington, and indeed in Western European capitals as well, that the Communist forces in

Greece were being directed by Moscow. Additionally, Turkey had been under Soviet pressure to agree to increased Soviet control over the straits providing access to the Black Sea. Aside from these and other increasingly numerous tension points between East and West, the Americans were becoming persuaded that a dangerous and fundamentally monolithic Communist *bloc* was developing which threatened the US and, more immediately, the still non-Communist but devastated nations of Western Europe. The Truman Doctrine declared universally and without reservation that the United States would assist "free peoples who are resisting attempted subjugation by armed minorities and by outside pressure". Some makers and observers of American foreign policy during that era, notably George Kennan, were unhappy with the approach, rightly seeing that it rather thoughtlessly and indiscriminately opened the door to all sorts of economic, diplomatic, and indeed military commitments around the globe. This, however, was not the dominant attitude in the United States government at that time. It was a period when informed opinion stressed the need to make as clear and unequivocal as possible the rejection of isolationism in favour of an active involvement in international affairs and acceptance of a range of foreign obligations.[19]

The Americans were exploring a new stance in international affairs; the British were withdrawing from obligations which were too heavy, including very historic ones in Southern Europe. The shift in responsibilities came quickly once it had been started. The US, not Britain, was the more prominent nation in denouncing continued Soviet military occupation of northern Iran, even though the initial movement of Soviet troops into the country had been part of a joint British–Russian agreement early in the Second World War. The US was anxious not to repeat previous errors of lack of concern with developments in and around Europe. From the British perspective, conflicts with the Americans over economic questions did not change the fact that the two nations were close allies. Entry of its more powerful associate into European affairs made it easier to yield to economic realities at home which could no longer be ignored.

FOREIGN POLICY DIRECTIONS

British economic problems hampered foreign policy, but did not result in abandonment of efforts to keep an important place in the constellation of nations. That a great nation had to pay close attention to foreign debts, trade balances and currency values was irritating to British statesmen accustomed to economic strength providing a secure base for international influence. "It does seem indeed hard," Churchill said in the early 1950s, "that the traditions and triumphs of a thousand years should be challenged by the ebb and flow of markets and commercial and financial transactions. . ."[20]

The nation's leaders were required to surrender important initiatives and responsibilities to the Americans, but remained determined to preserve a significant international role. British policy after the war remained loyal to historically consistent style. The keynote was flexibility; the guiding principle, protection of the national interest and global influence. Retreat from various outposts and obligations was conducted in piecemeal fashion, often in fact quite haphazardly. At the same time, the British ambitiously tried to operate on the three separate, demanding levels of relations with the United States and the Soviet Union, European nations, and Empire and Commonwealth. Significant attention was devoted to each; exclusive commitment was given to none. Relations concerning each level have been difficult as well as cordial over time. None of the spheres has been entirely satisfactory to Britain.

Close rapport with the US became the centrepiece of British foreign policy. The American cancellation of Lend-Lease was only one of several shocks to British–American relations after the war. The United States refused to share atomic energy plans with Britain on a bilateral basis, despite earlier steps toward doing so. Additionally, Truman's support for a Jewish state in Palestine and admission of more Jewish immigrants to the area without delay created consternation in British foreign policy circles.[21] Nevertheless, the British realised that the US was entering a period of very great international power and influence. The emerging superpower had already replaced the British in several parts of the world where tension with the Soviet Union was particularly intense. Cultural affinity joined with more dispassionate political calculation to lead the British to seek close ties. A series of personal relationships between leaders, ranging from very good to excellent, aided the association—Attlee and Truman, Churchill and Eisenhower, Macmillan and Kennedy.

Even while emphasising the special relationship with the US, British governments of both parties have made continuing efforts to maintain communication and seek better relations with the Soviet Union. The Attlee government tried hard to mitigate the trend toward growing tension between the Eastern and Western *blocs*. Directly after the war there was an effort, ultimately unsuccessful, to extend the term of the Anglo-Soviet treaty of 1942 from twenty to fifty years. The American alliance was the hub of British foreign policy, but like all such commitments was shaded by other considerations. Bevin was instrumental in forging close links with the US despite the difficulties which arose right after the war. At the same time, he had been known to speak of Britain as standing between its two wartime collaborators, helping to bring them together, in a particularly good position to find the key to East–West accommodation.[22]

British approaches to Europe have mixed involvement with independence. Britain has attempted generally to influence developments in Europe without becoming too closely entangled in them. A consistent theme of British statesmen during the years immediately after the war was that Europe was clearly secondary to the alliance with the US. In this sense, Churchill's famous declaration to de Gaulle, made during the war and quoted in the latter's memoirs, is revealing: "There is something you ought to know; each time we must choose between Europe and the open sea, we shall always choose the open sea. Each time I must choose between you and Roosevelt, I shall always choose Roosevelt!"[23]

After the war, Churchill became one of the foremost spokesmen for European integration. His prestige and rhetorical qualities guaranteed considerable attention to his remarks. Frequently he stated that a grand European federation was emerging, often mixing that conception with reference to closer ties across the Atlantic with the US, and around the world with the Commonwealth. For example, speaking at the Congress of the European movement in 1948, he appeared to view Europe and the British Empire as a single entity involved in "the gradual assumption of a larger sovereignty".[24]

Churchill's remarks served to complicate life for the Labour government and embarrassed its leaders. They suspected his activities were part of a Tory Party scheme to picture the government as old-fashioned and out of tune with emerging trends toward European and international unity. In fact, there was little real disagreement between leaders of the two parties concerning basic approaches to foreign policy. Any sacrifice of domestic sovereignty was anathema. Britain was anxious to involve the United States in protection of European security. Military pacts among the European states were encouraged. There was strong opposition, however, to any British involvement in movements for European political integration. Britain sought to encourage unity on the Continent while keeping a distinctive and quite independent position for itself.

Specific aspects of British policy reflected this general approach. The nation played a leading part in the formation of the NATO alliance and planning the administrative structure for receipt of US Marshall Plan economic aid. British fears that lack of Russian co-operation might delay or prevent Marshall Plan assistance led Bevin to move with great determination and speed, first to try to ensure their participation, and after that failed to work with France in constructing a plan for European reconstruction. In 1948, these efforts resulted in formation of the Organisation for European Economic Co-operation (OEEC), to distribute funds and oversee the recovery programme. In the same year, the Brussels Treaty was signed, involving Britain, Belgium, France, Luxembourg and the Netherlands in a defensive military pact. It also contained provisions for economic, cultural and social co-operation.[25]

Nevertheless, the British were equally anxious to avoid participation in organisations which would compromise national political sovereignty. Military co-ordination, and economic and other forms of general co-operation, were one thing; the formation of supranational economic and political institutions was quite another. Britain was a reluctant partner in the Council of Europe in 1949. In 1951, the British declined association with the European Coal and Steel Community, which involved a supranational administrative body. Britain refused to enter the European Economic Community in 1957. Indeed, British spokesmen frequently made disparaging and sarcastic references to the EEC, and an effort was made to counter it through the much looser European Free Trade Association.[26]

Very old traditions influenced British attitudes toward European integration; but there were also more specific considerations, including the belief that entry into Europe would change the significant relationship with the Commonwealth. Just as sentiment from the past led the nation to avoid close ties with Europe, so it has kept alive the hope for close continuing association with the diversity of states which comprise the Commonwealth. Britain has endeavoured to translate the history of colonial relationships into a co-operative global confederation of nations. It has been comparatively easy to maintain continuing links, thanks to the rather benign quality of British colonial policy, and the ease with which the nation surrendered its hold and granted independence after the Second World War. Indeed, the way in which Britain saw and accepted the strength of nationalist feelings in the colonies resulted in agreements for independence which contained, in many cases, pledges of continued military assistance and economic aid. The Empire has virtually disappeared, but significant burdens remain.

Overall, British foreign policy since the war has tried to employ dwindling national political, economic and military resources in maintaining an enormous range of international commitments. The contrast between British ambitions and capacities has encouraged sharp criticisms of that approach. Nevertheless, Britain's foreign policy record since the war has contained success as well as failure, examples of influence effectively brought to bear as well as of events which reflect British weakness and miscalculatioin.

There were a number of dramatic instances in which Britain influenced United States policy and developments in Europe. Britain's major role in the involvement of the US in European security arrangements is only one of several examples. During the Korean War, the British saw clearly the danger of clash with China and worked to restrain the United States. They also recognised the murky, complex character of the war in Indochina and helped to prevent US intervention after the French defeat in 1954. An effective intra-European catalyst in security matters, Britain persuaded its allies in the region— including France—to accept West German rearmament and entry into NATO. British leadership was important in arranging the Geneva Summit meeting of 1955. Throughout this period, the British remained true to their favoured flexibility. They saw more clearly than the Americans the growing difficulties with the Soviet Union at the end of and after the Second World War. In contrast to the US, Britain recognised the new communist regime in China soon after it took power.[27]

Britain's position became much weaker during the second half of the 1950s. The Suez crisis marks a major turning point in British–American relations, and consequently in Britain's international position. The resolution of the crisis revealed starkly that the two nations did not operate on a basis of equality. Prime Minister Eden tried to confront the Americans with a *fait accompli* in the coordinated British–French–Israeli attack on Egypt; instead, Eisenhower and Dulles showed that Britain's economic weakness and dependence provided a decisive lever for reversing its policy. Additionally, it was becoming increasingly clear that Britain could not longer keep up with the two superpowers in military capacity. The economic cost was simply too high. The Blue Streak missile, which had been planned as the central element in the British independent nuclear deterrent, was cancelled in 1960, underlining the point that Britain was slipping behind. In order to maintain a significant strategic capability, the British were forced into increasing dependence upon the Americans. The potential costs of this became real ones in 1962, when the Kennedy Administration cancelled the Skybolt missile. Skybolt, designed to be slung under the wings of bombers, was an important part of British plans to prolong the life of their nuclear deterrent. Ultimately, the crisis was resolved at the Nassau meeting at the end of the year, when Kennedy offered to substitute the Polaris missile. The British retained a nuclear capability, but had to accept even greater dependence on the US, as well as the acute embarrassment which attended the affair.[28]

In the years immediately after the war, when Britain's economic decline was not so apparent or severe, and its military strength was still very great, the special relationship with the US provided the nation with significant leverage on both sides of the Atlantic. Britain had the American ear, and this in turn facilitated influence in Europe without joining supranational institutions. Later, however, Britain's decline made her look more and more like an appendage rather than a partner of the Americans. The special cross-Atlantic tie which brought influence until the mid-1950s resulted in just the reverse later on. The Americans could take the British for granted, without fear of them breaking away from the Alliance in the manner of de Gaulle, or trying to open new doors to the East in the manner of the West Germans. British efforts at diplomatic initiative on the superpower level began to assume a futile, almost desperate quality. Various revealing images remain from efforts of Prime Ministers to play peacemakers: Macmillan journeying to Moscow during the winter in the late 1950s, his visit making little impact on either superpower; Wilson searching in the mid-1960s for a way to de-escalate the war in Vietnam, his efforts succeeding primarily in antagonising the Americans.

Unable to stay on a par with the US and the Soviet Union, Britain reversed earlier policy in 1961 and applied for membership in the Common Market. It was a dramatic departure from the British stance since the establishment of the EEC and also from a far older tradition of separation from Europe. The British could easily have entered the Community when it was formed. It is arguable whether or not a less antagonistic policy would have made eventual entry easier. British aloofness resulted in two humiliating rejections before entry was achieved in 1973.

Finally, while the Commonwealth continues to exist in a formal sense, and remains a focus for considerable British affection and attention, there has been little real political collaboration among the members. The nations involved are too disparate in their domestic regimes and foreign policies. They reflect the variety of the contemporary international system. Consequently, it has been impossible to transform the formal organisation into a working diplomatic coalition. With the exception of a few nations settled by very large numbers of British immigrants—Canada, Australia, New Zealand—there are no close, reliable links between Britain and the other Commonwealth nations. Even those three are more likely to turn to the US when significant military and security questions arise. Most members of the Commonwealth identify principally with their respective region, and beyond that with the non-white third world, rather than with the European nations which used to control them.

Commonwealth ties have created numerous problems for Britain. Kenyan and Rhodesian racial policies, for example, spurred ineffective British efforts to reform them. Kenya's expulsion of Asians holding British passports further complicated and intensified Britain's domestic racial problems. Once the decision was made to seek entry into the Common Market, trade obligations to Commonwealth nations had to be reconciled with the Community's rules. Residual defence commitments around the world have resulted in the stretching of British military capabilities more and more tightly to cover them. Indeed, the maintenance of a few ships or a tiny garrison far from home, in areas once ruled in part through threat of great military power, symbolises with irony the shrinking international position of the nation.

Reflecting on Britain's various international problems, critics have focused on these efforts to maintain many commitments in three distinctive spheres of foreign policy. Clearly, Britain would have had an easier time if the importance of entering Europe had been recognised earlier. Joining the Community when it was formed would have avoided the impression which developed later of British isolation between the two power centres of the United States and Europe. In a complementary manner, the British would have profited by putting less emphasis on increasingly tenuous links to the US and the Commonwealth. Britain has recognised the requirement of decline, but only slowly. Even when it was accepted, the British tried to accommodate by changing position somewhat rather than altering course to give European affairs clear emphasis over others.

Such points have considerable merit, but should not be overdrawn. Alternative approaches to British foreign policy carried potential costs as well as opportunities. The special relationship with the United States has been weakened in the sense that Britain is no longer on anything like an equal plane with the superpower, but it continues to exist in the area of close cultural ties, memories of wartime co-operation, and the habit of consultation on a range of topics. Britain could have joined the European Economic Community when it was formed, but later de Gaulle's attitude ensured that application to enter would be greeted with suspicion and hostility. It should be kept in mind in this connection that the French President's suggestion early in his rule for an Atlantic "directorate" of France, Britain and the United States was made outside the EEC context. It is at least possible that a less reluctant effort by Britain to join would have damaged the abstract but important relationship with the Americans. More clearly, while the Commonwealth may not provide Britain with significant international influence, abruptly terminating existing economic arrangements in order to join Europe would doubtless have fostered enmity toward Britain and disrupted many of the economies involved.

More important, there is the underlying point that decisiveness itself, quick movements and rapid shifts in foreign policy historically has not been the British style. Rather, subtlety, ambiguity, compromise and gradual adjustment have been the principal features. Total clarity in policy and position have been sacrificed in order to accomodate various competing viewpoints and interests. It is precisely this quality which led to Britain's comparative moderation and restraint when it was at the height of international economic and military power. Since the Second World War, Britain's adjustment to much reduced status has been slow but also steady and generally in tune with changing power relationships. Britain accepted the Americans' penumbra, binding the much more powerful ally closely to Europe and keeping open a channel of communication which was important if not always successfully employed. The necessity to join Europe was recognised, even if belatedly. The Empire was abandoned reluctantly, but with far less violence and resistance to change than was the case with other European colonial powers. Decline in international influence has been handled in the same way as the earlier assumption of a global role, moderately and with attention to the need for stability. Waltz makes the same point after outlining the various, generally unco-ordinated ways in which Britain has moved to accept current realities: ". . . most of these are not inspiring ways of adjusting to decline in a country's international status, but they are benign."[29]

STRESS ON A SHRINKING ECONOMIC BASE

Since economic conditions have been a primary source of Britain's international difficulties, they deserve explicit consideration and discussion. It is appropriate to discuss them early, as a prelude to analysis of Britain's policy and institutional responses to the changed international environment. In decades past, the nation's international power rested upon an enormous economic base. The first economy to undergo the industrial revolution, the dominant commercial power until late in the nineteenth century, energetic in building up domestic capacity and conquering an empire of raw materials, Britain used vast wealth to gain influence. Thanks to British shrewdness, these substantial assets were frequently employed with considerable political skill.

This situation began to change even before the turn of the century. Other nations developed their own industrial capacities. Germany and the United States were especially important in providing increasingly strong challenges to British industry. From at least the last quarter of the nineteenth century, it was clear that Britain was beginning to fall behind these other countries. In 1872, Britain's share of the world export trade began to diminish, despite heavy dependence on imports of food and raw materials. By the turn of the century, the nation had dropped from first place to third in steel production. Cotton textiles, which were among the most important British manufactured goods, were no longer being exported to the United States and other European countries in enormous quantities. Britain was exporting increasing amounts of machinery, and importing a growing proportion of essential food supplies. Farming was declining in Britain during the same period that vast expanses of the American heartland were being thrown open to cultivation.[30]

Economic decline became more noticeable after the First World War, and much more serious still after the Second World War. The British economy enjoyed no American-style boom in the 1920s. From 1921 until the onset of the Second World War, unemployment remained high. Changing governments, primarily Conservative or Conservative-dominated, struggled rather ineffectually to improve the situation.[31] After the war, economic weakness could no longer be ignored in the definition of foreign policy commitments. Constant preoccupation with the balance of payments, and the frustration of a quickening domestic economic pace leading to an unfavourable imbalance, have provided the dominant motif of postwar policy-making.

The Second World War brought enormous problems. It actually led to much greater production, but also to an economy organised for the manufacture of goods needed for the war effort. In consequence, there was need for considerable industrial adjustment after the war. Vast amounts of wealth were lost through destruction of housing, plants and equipment, ships and cargoes. The export industries, vital to economic wellbeing, were starved for manpower. There was a great deal of demand built up for consumer goods, leading to some tension with the goal of focusing on those industries most appropriate to the export market.[32]

Britain also ended the war heavily in debt. The burden resulted principally from costs of maintaining troops and military installations in various parts of the globe. Only some of the expense had been met through Lend-Lease or overseas earnings and sales. In consequence, this foreign debt expanded from £476 million in August 1939 to £3355 million in June 1945. Funding and attempting to reduce this very large total liability was to be a major preoccupation of British policy-makers after the war.[33]

The British received a particularly severe and offensive economic shock with the abrupt American termination of Lend-Lease in August 1945. The economic effect of the decision was overshadowed by its psychological impact. The decision was made without consultation, even though Britain had been the recipient of over two-thirds of the Lend-Lease aid distributed during the war. There was, moreover, a picayune quality to the American cancellation, with insistence on payment for supplies in transit, just arrived, or waiting to be delivered. Technically, the statute governing the programme prohibited its continuation after the end of hostilities. Nevertheless, the Truman Administration could have undertaken to ease these conditions. In Britain, there were strong suspicions that the Americans were purposely making life hard, thanks to a combined dislike of the new Labour government and continuing British attachment to the old-fashioned Empire. From the American perspective, different considerations carried weight. After all, the war was over, the Cold War had not yet settled over Europe, and many Americans remembered bitterly European failure to repay First World War debts. The Second World War had been costly for the Americans as well, and there was no doubt at least a whiff of traditional disdain for the Europeans and their propensity for diplomatic competition and military conflicts.[34]

The US offered to assist Britain in managing and reducing economic difficulties, but the required price was high. Rather than modifying the conditions for Lend-Lease, the Americans chose to offer the British low-interest loans, tied, however, to terms which were guaranteed to open British trading areas to other nations. Britain was compelled to make sterling freely convertible to other currencies, to agree not to discriminate against American goods, and to open export markets to the US. As part of the general agreement, Britain was to accept and work within the international monetary institutions negotiated at Bretton Woods in 1944. The Americans were showing determination not only to remain significantly involved in international affairs, but also to press for national advantages and acceptance of their conception of an appropriate postwar economic order. British bitterness was deeply felt. Epstein, for example, describes the reaction in Labour circles:

> In the general argument against American economic policy made by Harold Wilson [a spokesman for the party's left], the "abrupt withdrawal" of aid was discussed in the context of Britain's plight in having lost export markets, especially during the war, to the United States. The Americans, in this portrait, re-emerged as the direct beneficiaries of Britain's sacrificial wartime losses.[35]

When a great industrial power declines, especially in such a dramatic fashion, more than one factor is likely to be important in providing an explanation, and this is true here. At least three considerations should be touched upon in any effort to understand present difficulties. First, Britain has always been unusually dependent upon imports. Second, while the British industrial revolution took place early, the rate of national economic growth has never been very high. Third, features of social life in Britain appear to have had an effect in weakening economic growth, productivity and innovation.[36]

The need to import means that Britain's economy was in one sense precarious even when it was dominant internationally. As a small island nation, with little in the way of natural resources, trade was essential to survival. The nation's economic power was based on assets of skill and ingenuity rather than domestic raw materials. As long as Britain's industrial supremacy was unchallenged, and overseas areas provided sufficient cheap raw materials, there was little incentive to be concerned. Even at the height of the nation's power, nevertheless, economic prosperity rested on a peculiarly fragile base.

The requirement to import means there is pressure to export as well, and here the British economy has not performed well since the Second World War. It should be kept in mind that London historically has been a major international financial centre, providing important "invisible" earnings, notably in insurance. Nevertheless, the British have still been confronted by chronic unfavourable balances of payments since the Second World War, and to some extent before that. This continuing problem has threatened the value of the pound, and at times has brought acute financial crisis, with the ominous threat of insolvency. Among other things, payments deficits have hampered and restricted economic growth, thanks to government efforts to limit imports.

From another related perspective, growth should be considered separately. As with the need to import, slow growth historically has been a feature of the British economy. More recently, it has become as well a source of serious concern and difficulty. The problem of British growth has been, basically, an inability to keep up with competing industrial nations. This has led some to infer that the British economy has been comparatively sluggish in recent years. Actually, the situation is more subtle and complex. British economic strength and prosperity resulted not from rapid growth, but from very consistent growth over a very long period of time. Historical data are not totally reliable, but nevertheless do provide general outlines of changes over time. The evidence indicates strongly that, from the very start of the British industrial revolution in the 1780s, economic growth has been steady but fairly slow by the standards of other modern western industrial nations. Status as the first industrial economy should not be confused with a rapid growth rate. Britain was in the lead because of an enormous head start, not as a result of particularly great speed in running the race. Moreover, in comparison with other periods, the British economy has actually performed rather well during postwar decades. During 1955–65, growth was 2.5 per cent per year, a rate matched in the past only in the 1870s and 1880s.[37]

Along with the problems of slow growth, it is customary to identify general lack of innovation and managerial complacency as important, if comparatively abstract, problems of the British economy. Plant and equipment have allegedly been allowed to grow old without being replaced. Increasing competition from abroad has not been met by new techniques and methods of production. To be sure, such general statements are easy to make but hard to quantify, and should therefore be handled with caution. Professional economists, with characteristic dislike of arguments which cannot be based on clean and concrete data, are often sceptical of such observations. The principal author of a rather comprehensive Brookings Institution study on the state of the

British economy, for example, outlines the standard arguments about the spread of complacency and absence of innovation, ending with a whiff of scorn: "This dark fable, bardic with years of telling, recurs regularly today to explain low efficiency and slow growth in the British economy."[38] Nevertheless, throughout this book technical economic analysis is joined by reference to the influence of general social and cultural attitudes. The same author notes later that British management has been hampered by amateurism. Greater admiration for the civil service than for business among managers has apparently fostered "a trustee role of gentlemanly responsiblity" rather than one of activism and innovation. And the final paragraph of the volume contains the following rhetorical summary observation, drawing on the essays which precede it: "Does economic advice here overstep into social imperative? Are we not propounding growth and change in a society where don and docker alike prefer tradition, leisure and stability? This may be."[39]

Each of the basic factors—high dependence upon imports, traditionally slow growth, and attitudes of complacency—is useful in understanding the decline of Britain from industrial leader to one of the most problem-ridden of Western economies. If there has been a deterioration in the quality of management, this would obviously be an important shift from earlier periods. On the other hand, more concrete factors in the British economy have not changed. Rather, the more general environment has been transformed. Slow growth and dependence upon raw materials from overseas have been characteristic of Britain historically, but only in comparatively recent times have they created economic difficulties. The Empire is gone, other industrial powers have emerged. The economic world has changed drastically; Britain in important ways has not.

THE BRITISH RESPONSE

Continuity of basic features of the economy does not mean there was no British reaction to the gradually worsening economic situation. On the contrary, the twentieth century witnessed serious efforts to protect British markets and access to raw materials. Under pressures generated by stiff competition, the British moved away from their traditional free trade practices and toward more explicit special links with the Commonwealth. Liberal notions of the beneficial returns from very low or non-existent trade barriers won a significant victory with the repeal of the Corn Laws in 1846, an event cited often and rightly as a major breakthrough for free trade advocates. Thereafter, liberal economics, with its faith in open competition, became strongly rooted in official policy.

Nevertheless, there was a marked change after the Second World War. Facing economic difficulties which were gradually but steadily growing worse at home, plus nationalistic reactions in other countries, the British moved in clearly protectionistic directions. Domestic agriculture was subsidised. Tariffs were raised on foreign agricultural products and some manufactured goods as well. At the same time, steps were taken to establish Imperial (later Commonwealth) Preference. This refers to the system of special trade agreements among Commonwealth nations to facilitate sale of British manufactured goods in return for purchase of food and raw materials from other members. The immediate incentives were of course economic, and significant preference arrangements were worked out during the Great Depression in the 1930s. However, there were other motives as well. Many in Britain viewed the system as a way to provide important political and economic cohesion to the diverse Commonwealth. The end of Empire therefore would not mean the termination of a global imperial role.[40]

Such ambitions were great, and ultimately proved hollow. The concerted effort to encourage Commonwealth trade and build walls against the rest of the industrial world created too many problems. Preferences were not advantageous to all the nations that might have participated, and protectionism was never pursued really vigorously. Ultimately, when it became clear after the Second World War that Commonwealth Preference was unlikely to establish a strong and coherent trading network, the British moved in other directions. Again, although perhaps guilty of unrealistic ambitions, they cannot be accused of pursuing them rigidly or unbendingly. The scheme had been viewed as important, but nevertheless was abandoned fairly painlessly.

Flexibility is not the same as foresight, however, and it was apparent soon after the war that Britain's overall economic position was growing weaker. There was no dramatic relief from wartime stringencies. The economy benefited from the immediate postwar surge in demand for labour, and unemployment was low. Nevertheless, it proved very difficult to satisfy both consumer demand, which had built up during six years of wartime sacrifice, and the requirement for substantial exports to balance imports. Britain was forced to borrow more and more funds abroad in order to avoid insolvency.[41]

In the context of this worrisome economic situation, the 1946–7 winter in Britain was exceptionally harsh. The bad weather symbolised the growing economic plight and created a number of immediate concrete problems. It led to a depletion of fuel supplies. Power was rationed, both for industrial and home use. This in turn resulted in a temporary increase in unemployment, and created a significant new psychological burden for a population which had already gone through considerable hardship. Beyond these specific developments, the winter crisis also drew attention to more deeply rooted economic problems. As an historian of the period notes: "Nature aggravated the problem but did not create it. No economy was sound which could not withstand a couple of months of bad weather. The trouble was the lagging production, the slowdowns in mines and factories, the low stocks of fuels."[42] These specific shortages and shortcomings reflected the more basic dilemma that low productivity, combined with an economy drained by wartime demands, left no margin to use in getting through the short-term problems brought by the severe winter.

The winter crisis resulted in a number of efforts by Clement Attlee's Labour government to strengthen the economy and increase productivity. In effect, the weather joined with the attitude of the American government to emphasise the seriousness of the economic situation. Measures included establishing general priority goals for exports, planning allocation of raw materials, and termination of the convertibility of sterling. Although there were also plans to control allocations of labour, they were never implemented. Government policy did enjoy some brief success. There was an especially significant victory in the struggle to hold down inflation. For two years, from 1948 to 1950, co-operation among government, business and labour effectively prevented prices and wages from rising. The key element was willingness of unions to forego wage increases. This was achieved through a combination of direct appeal and other policies designed to restrain food prices, impose a levy on capital, and limit dividends. More broadly, gains were made in 1948 to reduce the balance-of-payments deficit, and there was growth in exports, national income and industrial production.[43]

Successful wage and price restraint, however, proved to be short-lived. In 1949, there was significant deterioration in the nation's international economic position. The main problem was one which would continue to plague economic policy after the war—the balance of payments, and more specifically at this time the dollar account. The dollar deficit rose as the year progressed. At the same time, the United States reduced aid to Britain. Reflecting the basic weakness of the British economy, this shift in payments position had very substantial domestic reverberations. Again, events made the point that the nation was operating on a very narrow economic margin. As a result of these pressures, the pound in 1949 was devalued by thirty per cent. Devaluation in turn generated demands at home for wage and price increases, which eventually broke down the alliance between government and major producer groups which had temporarily checked inflation.

The chronic problem of balance-of-payments deficits, combined with lack of substantial currency reserves, has led to the continuing phenomenon of "stop–go" economic policies at home. When the British economy expands, this consistently results in significantly increased demands for imports, thus worsening the balance-of-payments position. Successive governments have been forced to apply brakes to the economy, using various combinations of fiscal, monetary and incomes policy. This has temporarily alleviated balance-of-payments difficulties, but has also led to recession—a halt in growth and rise in unemployment.

During the period right after the war, Britain's economic problems led to considerable wrangling between and within the political parties. The Conservatives bitterly criticised the government's industrial nationalisation programme, though later essentially accepted the significant social and economic reforms which had been instituted. The left wing of the Labour Party tried to take advantage of the crisis to bring about far-reaching changes in foreign policy, away from close association with the United States and toward a more neutral stance. Attlee and his colleagues struggled to address the deepseated economic difficulties, in an atmosphere of bitterness which was fed by the very realisation of the seriousness of the situation. Doubtless the continuing economic strains contributed to the significant Labour losses in the 1950 general election, and to the clear Conservative victory in 1951.[44]

Economic problems eased somewhat in the 1950s. There was an improvement in the balance-of-payments situation. This, however, was not due to any basic change in the structural characteristics of the British economy or the nation's position in the wider economic world. Rather, it was related to beneficial shifts in the global economy, specifically to a relative drop in the prices of commodities. Temporary calm did not mean that anything resembling basic security had been restored.

Indeed, through the 1960s Britain's economic position gradually but fairly steadily grew weaker. There was another devaluation of the pound in November 1967, from $2.80 to $2.40. Once again, this was an effort to relieve, at least temporarily, increasingly unfavourable payments balances. Aside from payments accounts, a continuing problem has been inflationary pressures within the economy. This in turn has reflected the inability of successive governments to achieve working agreements among management and labour to hold down wage and price rises. Inflation has weakened the nation's international economic position, rendering products less competitive abroad and the domestic economy more vulnerable to penetration by foreign enterprise. In retrospect, the effective collaboration of 1948–50 among diverse interests to manage the economy marks a high point of success for public policy in this field since the war. The Conservative governments of the 1950s tried but failed to produce similar accord. Instead, the Macmillan regime was forced to rely upon fiscal and monetary tools to hold down demand and therefore prices. This proved only a temporary expedient. By the early 1960s, policy-makers were again confronting serious balance-of-payments deficits and rising prices.

An important element in the economic calculus has been the increasingly serious nature of industrial conflict. The Conservative and Labour governments of recent years have experimented with various efforts to plan the economy in a direct manner, including such innovations as the National Economic Development Council (established by the Conservatives in 1962) and the Department of Economic Affairs (established by Labour in 1964). Other initiatives included the effort by the Wilson government to control strikes by statute, and the Heath government's wage–price control experiment. Neither proved successful. Indeed, the Wilson plan resulted in intense strife within the Labour Party, which ultimately forced him to withdraw it from consideration by Parliament.[45]

More recently still, during the recent Wilson government, there was an effort to bring about voluntary wage restraint by means of what has been termed the "social contract". Its purpose was to persuade trade unions to restrict wage demands to levels no higher than the increase in the cost of living. The plan was subjected to a great deal of sceptical criticism, especially from conservative business-oriented quarters such as the journal *The Economist*. Ultimately, the contract's ceiling was pierced so often that it had to be abandoned. In its place, Wilson brought forth a new scheme in which wage increases were to be restricted to a maximum of £6 per week.

These various efforts have represented the continuing struggle of successive governments to wrestle effectively with the horns of a great dilemma. On the one hand, it has proved impossible to implement a statutory wage control policy. On the other, it is imperative to try to control the spiral of wage inflation. A large acceleration of the rate occurred in 1970, when wage increases approached an annual rate of twenty per cent, and prices went up by over ten per cent. While startling at the time, this development was overshadowed by what came later. By 1974, the annual rate of inflation had reached a level of approximately twenty-five per cent.

The seriousness of economic problems in Britain has several important implications for foreign policy analysis. It is appropriate to discuss this set of issues early in the study, for they have coloured, influenced and helped to define several major dimensions of British foreign policy since the Second World War. Generally, economic conditions have meant that the domestic base from which foreign policy is conducted has been weak and appears to be growing weaker. Moreover, full awareness in Britain of the significance of economic decline has come only recently. In more specific terms, growing economic problems changed the nature of the Anglo-American tie from partnership to dependence. A link which had once increased British standing changed to one highlighting vulnerability. Because Britain was so dependent economically on the United States, an automatic source of control was placed in the hands of the stronger partner. British retreat from an extensive international role, and the accompanying shift toward Europe, again were responses to the dictates of economic realities.

2 Political Culture, Institutions and Practices

British retreat from old policies and commitments has been gradual. Only slowly has the reality been accepted that the nation can no longer be a global power and must be content with more modest status. As long as possible, the British held to the notion that a position of something resembling equality with the two superpowers could be maintained. Part of the explanation for reluctance to abandon traditional stances in international relations was that they actually worked quite well for a number of years following the Second World War. At least until the Suez disaster of 1956, it was possible for the British to believe they could play an independent role, linking Europe to the US while remaining closely bound to neither. Similarly, until the 1960s Britain retained control over a still substantial colonial empire.

Nevertheless, attachment to the ambition for a global role outlasted national capabilities to maintain it. When retreat occurred, it was gradual and largely unplanned, not the reflection of a basic conscious re-evaluation of the position of the nation. Contraction of obligations has been conducted in response to external pressures, which have been primarily economic, rather than to internal comprehensive policy planning. As the following chapters describe, this general quality of British foreign policy is reflected as well in specific approaches to the European Economic Community and defence policy. Gradualism, slow adjustment and flexibility have characterised policies on both general and specific levels.

Political culture, and institutional structures and practices, have an important bearing on this overall quality of foreign policy. It is general cultural attitudes which define approaches to international affairs and the parameters of policy. The organisation of politics and government channels sentiment into policy, working in the process to promote consensus or cleavage, unity or disarray. Discussion in this chapter will consider the attitudes underlying political behaviour, the manner in which political competition and public policy development occur, and the specific sectors of government involved in foreign policy. Comparisons and contrasts are made with the United States, as one device for highlighting particular strengths and weaknesses of British approaches to foreign policy organisation.

Generally, it is accurate to state that patterns of continuity have been as typical of British domestic politics as they have of foreign policy. Just as the English Channel provided military security to Britain, so the nation's political institutions were sheltered from the more violent and disruptive currents of Continental politics. The French Revolution reverberated in decades of violence and instability within Europe. While Britain was involved heavily in the resulting wars and diplomacy, its domestic institutions retain their stability. Over the last several centuries, Continental states have been created and destroyed, had their borders changed, been occupied and liberated, and seen their political regimes transformed. Britain has influenced such events without falling victim to them.

British politics has shown capacity for change and reform, but normally within the context of gradual adjustment rather than abrupt departures from the past. The English experienced civil war in the seventeenth century, and there have been political disruptions and rebellions of various sorts from that period to the present. Some conflicts, such as the long and bitter one between England and Ireland, have been quite severe. Additionally, there have been exceptionally active reformist governments, notably the Liberal regime which took office in 1906 and the Labour government elected in 1945. Nevertheless, rather than overthrowing traditional practices and institutions, change has been accommodated to them. A revolutionary tradition did not follow from the civil war; there was, instead, a conservative reaction. Since the restoration of the monarchy in the 1660s it has gradually grown weaker but has not been abolished. The House of Lords has become secondary to the Commons, and both have in recent decades been overshadowed by Cabinet and Prime Ministerial power. However, these changes have taken place over a long period of time, and Parliament remains an important arena for debate and influence on the government of the day, even if it no longer makes and unmakes Cabinets. In a similar manner, the electoral suffrage has been extended from a comparatively small aristocracy to include virtually the entire adult population; but the process has been gradual for over a century, involving a number of limited reform statutes rather than a single sweeping change.

The term political culture refers to the attitudes and beliefs of a population which are significant for political behaviour. In recent years, it has become common for political scientists to focus on this dimension of a political system, often undertaking to analyse survey data in the process. British political culture continues to be impressive in its stability; the population is hardly passive, but rather mixes respect for established institutions and customs with political assertiveness. Gabriel Almond and Sidney Verba, in the pathbreaking study of political culture in five democratic nations, *The Civic Culture*, were impressed by the degree to which the British political system maintained a stable tension between notions of rights and obligations of citizens, between respect for public institutions and desire to assert the public will. They cite the conclusions of two other recent but less quantitative observers to bolster their case:

> [D. W.] Brogan points out that in the historical development of Britain the culture of democratic citizenship, with its emphasis on initiative and participation, was amalgamated with an older political culture that stressed the obligations and rights of the subjects. [Harry] Eckstein points out that the British political culture combines deference toward authority with a lively sense of the rights of citizen initiative. [1]

The nature of British political culture bears upon the conduct of foreign policy in at least two ways. First, the essential stability of the nation's politics has meant that foreign policy has been conducted from a secure base. Cabinet ministers have considerable freedom to define and carry out policy, knowing that if it fails a government may fall, but that the institutions of government are unlikely to be toppled. Suez brought the end of the Eden government, and doubtless contributed to a self-critical and divisive national mood, but it did not carry the threat of revolution or an overturning of the past. Indeed, the Macmillan government which followed was able to make foreign policy decisions confidently, unhindered by the effects of Suez, even though Macmillan had served as Chancellor of the Exchequer with the former Prime Minister. [2]

Second, the moderation of British politics has been reflected in the character of foreign policy. This is not to deny the presence of serious conflicts over specific policies. There have been quite sharp rifts within both major parties, especially Labour. The continuing cleavage between the Labour left and the rest of the party has had a foreign policy dimension. In the 1950s it concerned unilateral disarmament; more recently it has involved the issue of continued membership in the

Common Market. Factionalism has been less pronounced in the Conservative Party, but Suez is nevertheless not the only occasion in recent years when there have been serious internal party strains. Levels of defence expenditure, involvement in Europe, and the importance of Empire and Commonwealth are subjects which have all caused serious difficulties, if not actual factional splits. Additionally, a continuing philosophical and emotional gulf separates the parties. Debate in the House of Commons often approaches levels of hostility and bitter sarcasm which are quite rare in the US Congress. Nevertheless, the intensity of party competition exists within a larger framework of compromise, accomodation and gradual change. Major shifts in domestic policy, whether they have involved the extension of the suffrage, broadening of educational opportunities, or nationalisation of a sector of the economy, have tended to be incremental rather than abrupt. In the same manner, it is not surprising that British adjustments to a changing international environment have been slowmoving and, at least in some respects, indecisive. Britain's position after the Second World War did not compel a drastic re-evaluation of power and role in the international system. It is clear also that the style and traditions under which political change generally has occurred in Britain likewise discouraged sharp departures from the past.

Methods of recruitment into positions of power in parties and government encourage conformity to established practices, sensitivity to the views of colleagues, and general caution. Cabinet members, including the Prime Minister, reach the summit only after long years of party service. The key to success in British national politics is to start early and diligently move up into and through the hierarchy in a conventional manner. As a result, Prime Ministers have generally been at least middle-aged upon reaching the summit. Just as important, they have been through a long process of acculturation and socialisation. Similarly, Cabinet members share the basic characteristic of long service in the wellworn grooves of established party office. It is unlikely that leadership produced by such methods will engage in very significant departures from the *status quo,* and this expectation has been borne out by the conduct of British government. What is sacrificed, naturally, is the likelihood of innovation, novelty and striking departures in policy.

The selection of political leadership is handled very differently in the United States, a point often made by students of the two political systems, and important enough to be repeated here. Presidential candidates of the major parties have represented a variety of generational levels and professional backgrounds. Eisenhower and Willkie, two who had an especially marked and dramatic public impact—one enormously successful electorally, the other equally unsuccessful—were not conventional party politicians at all. The former was from the military, the latter from business. It is in Congress that there is a power structure which resembles the British approach to leadership selection, at least in established customs and procedures if not personal styles. Power is accumulated through years of conformity to the hierarchy, combined with astute judgement and ability to manoeuvre in the background in terms of being selected for the right committee posts. It was the similarity in power and relationship to the head of government which led Richard Neustadt to draw a perceptive parallel between British Cabinet members and the leaders and committee chairmen of Congress.[3]

There remains, of course, a very large gulf between power in Congress and the achievement of the Presidency. Most who are powerful in the legislative environment never take the step of seeking the highest executive office, although there has been a trend in recent decades for Senators to become more prominent that Governors as presidential candidates. The main point is that power in the Congressional milieu does not readily or easily translate into success in the presidential arena. Lyndon Johnson, the dominant figure in the US Senate at the time, was defeated for the 1960 Democratic nomination by John Kennedy, who was not a significant force in Congress. This is an especially strong example, which nevertheless illustrates a valid general point.

In recent years, there has been an important debate about whether or not the balance of forces in British government—and therefore in political life as well—is changing. The observation is often made that Prime Ministerial power is becoming so great that Cabinet government is steadily being transformed into something resembling the American presidential system. Certainly the electronic media have given the Prime Minister a visibility and prominence within the nation which was previously impossible. This does tend to focus increased popular attention on the personality, habits and style of the head of government. In turn, this naturally has encouraged drawing parallels with the United States, where the Presidency has traditionally involved public interest in the man occupying the office as well as in his institutional functions. More substantially, the modern Prime Minister has significant resources at his disposal. These include extensive patronage, power to appoint Cabinet colleagues, and control over the

Cabinet committee structure, agenda and staff support. The power of the Prime Minister, in tandem with the comparative freedom of government leaders which is traditional in Britain, might be considered a combination likely to lead to dominance of policy by the head of government.[4]

In fact, however, there are various important restraints operating on the Prime Minister, which guarantee that the office will continue to be different from—and in important respects more limited than—that of the President of the United States. An American President has a Cabinet which serves at his pleasure and a range of possible initiatives which he can take independently of Congressional approval. Nevertheless, no President wants to have symbolic resignations from his Cabinet if they can be avoided, and an aroused Congress has various tools which can be employed to investigate the Executive and control its budget. The Prime Minister is even more seriously restricted, though in more subtle ways. If a Prime Minister is wise, he must endeavour to ensure that political decisions reflect the views of a large part of the Cabinet, especially when major issues are at stake. In contrast to the situation in the United States, British Cabinet ministers are important and powerful party figures. Cabinet decisions may formally be collective, requiring every minister to support them, but members of a government can still threaten to resign and actually carry out the threat. A Prime Minister who forces a decision upon powerful Cabinet colleagues may find a much larger coalition opposing him the next time a controversial matter arises. The British Cabinet system, therefore, puts a major emphasis on reaching preliminary consensus early, before tensions get out of hand, or at times even before they are clearly defined.

More generally, in terms of party politics, members of a British government are under strong pressure to remain in contact with backbench opinion in their parliamentary party. Again, practices contrast with the distance automatically present between President and Congress in the US. MPs may have lost the nineteenth-century power to overturn Cabinets, but they can still criticise and revolt against their party. The strength of contemporary party discipline is often emphasised. It is important that it is not exaggerated. If the party is badly split, there is little the leadership can do to impose unity. In reality, there is considerable consultation between party leaders and backbenchers, involving give and take by both sides. This occurs whether or not a party is in power; when in government, party leaders might have very important levers of patronage at their disposal, but at the same time sharp internal splits are also especially embarrassing. Samuel Beer has noted in a recent general work on British politics and government, "On few generalizations do former Ministers agree more than on their report of the constant, anxious, and even deferential attention Cabinets give to the opinions of their backbenchers."[5]

Characteristics of governmental decision-making and interchange generally which bear on foreign policy underline the important differences between Britain and the US. There are great pressures within British government for consensus and accommodation, for establishing positions which are broadly acceptable rather than risking sharp cleavages among powerful individuals and groups. This is not only true for senior and junior party figures serving in government posts, but also for the civil servants who play an important part in the preparation of choices and the implementation following decision. There is considerable contrast here between Britain and the United States. In the former country, development of public policy involves a great deal of private consultation, using informal but reliable channels of interchange among officials who have established links over years of close personal association. The American style, on the other hand, is more open, obvious and competitive, with alliances constantly having to be reforged to fight new battles.

Doubtless part of the reason is that the scale of government administration is so much larger in the United States. Washington contains a vast bureaucratic apparatus, and this observation applies in the area of foreign affairs just as it does to public policy as a whole. In recent years, there has been a very substantial reorganisation, modernisation and expansion of administrative structures in British government, along what can rightly be termed American lines. Moreover, the foreign service personnel in both countries are comparatively small numerically (see Table 2.1). Nevertheless, and especially in view of the current great involvement of domestic agencies in international concerns, it remains true that there is a substantial discrepancy in sheer scale between those sectors of the two bureaucracies involved in foreign policy.

Socially and psychologically, the world of government in Britain is more closed, intense and limited than in the US. In London, civil service life is made up of a complex and highly efficient network based upon personal relationships, confidence and histories of professional association between particular individuals. This means that positions on policy in Britain are established through accommodation and conciliation, a process which occurs informally over lunch and in the

TABLE 2.1   *Diplomatic Service Personnel: United States and Britain*

1. *Britain*

	At home	Abroad	Total diplomatic service
Administrative class	400	700	1100
Executive class	900	1000	1900
Totals	1300	1700	3000

2. *United States*

Executive/programme direction	342
Political	1210
Economic/commercial	813
Subtotal, substantive personnel	2365
Consular	484
Administrative	608
Special (medical, etc.)	8
Total	3465

(Sources: *Report of the Review Committee on Overseas Representation,* 1968–1969, Sir Val Duncan Chrmn., Cmnd. 4107 (July 1969); *Commission on the Organization of the Government for the Conduct of Foreign Policy* (June 1975), US Government Printing Office, p. 176, figures for US as of December 1974)

corridors as much as it does at formal meetings. In Washington, coalitions on important matters are built up only by surmounting a number of hurdles, including the hostility and suspicion of other sectors of the bureaucracy. Alliances are fragile and subject to disruption. Old barriers constantly have to be surmounted as new issues arise. In London, support once established is more easily maintained.[6]

Reflecting these different environments, personnel change is much greater in the United States. With the advent of a new presidential administration, turnover normally reaches levels well below the Cabinet. Kenneth Waltz stresses this point in his comparative study of British and American foreign policy, and notes also that there has often been substantial turnover during the course of a single presidential administration adding that this appears to be far from damaging. During the period immediately after the Second World War, there was a complete change in holders of important positions in the State Department. But this does not appear to have been unhealthy; rather, the same period is generally regarded as a time of especially effective leadership by State, when the Department was able to guide the rest of the government, and thus the nation, through the difficult postwar transition.[7]

Waltz does an effective job of contrasting these American practices with the British tendency to keep all but a few civil servants in the same department through their careers, while at the same time choosing officials at the very highest levels from a small and very continuous group of party leaders. He states: "Despite the low prestige of public service and the small monetary rewards it brings, no government approaches the American record, established in and after the New Deal, for drawing into its service so many men from the higher levels of business and the professions." The advantages of new outlooks are obvious: "Turnover of personnel refreshes the bureaucracy by bringing in people from outside the government." Waltz rightly sees movement of people within the government as a source of co-ordination, but there is also no doubt that frequent interchange of public officials with outside organisations creates a more open as well as more uncertain system.[8]

These various political and administrative differences between the two countries create great contrasts in the style of and approach to policy-making generally, as well as in the actual content of policies. This general observation involves foreign as well as domestic affairs. In one sense, British decision-makers have a good deal of independence. The political culture is stable, with strong traditions of legitimacy for duly elected authority. The unitary character of government does not put formal, obvious barriers in the path of those at the top. To choose one example among many, treaties in the US must be ratified by the Senate. There is no such constitutional obligation on British governments. Technically, the Monarch approves such agreements and by so doing brings them into effect. In practice, however, this freedom of British leaders is restricted by a political culture which encourages modesty in departures from the *status quo,* and by informal customs and procedures which place a premium on accommodation among various groups and individuals, wide consultation and mutual influence, and long apprenticeship before the summit of power is reached. In the United States, the course of executive leadership is much more uncertain and unpredictable. The system runs the risk of erratic policy and inexperienced men entering high office. Additionally, the existence of various power centres makes it more difficult to implement policy smoothly once it has been decided upon. Here too, however, the situation means among other things that policy may be highly innovative, with all the risks for both positive accomplishment and disastrous failure which this implies.

Given these many differences, it is not surprising that the general approaches to foreign policy in the two countries have been quite distinctive. The United States has, in very broad terms, moved into a position of great international leadership comparable to that which Britain formerly occupied. The ways in which each has accommodated to new status, however, have been quite different. After the Second World War the Americans, aware of their enormous power and sensitive to mistakes of the past, were determined to play a significant international role. After some initial vacillation, a firm commitment was consciously made to involvement in alliances with European and, eventually, other foreign powers. In a short period of time, a tradition of isolation was reversed. Britain, on the other hand, has gone through a much slower and more gradual withdrawal, prodded and driven by events rather than being guided by a comprehensive view of the world and the nation's role within it. Aside from the strength of a basic tradition of incremental change, there has been little in the institutional structures or practices of British politics to encourage exposure of those in power to heretical ideas or significant shifts in the *status quo*.

ADMINISTRATION OF FOREIGN POLICY

Politicians define basic policies in the Cabinet context, but administrators implement the decision made. Moreover, civil servants, formally removed from the arena of party political competition, still have a major role in the development of public policy. In consequence, it is important to examine the administrative as well as political and cultural contexts in which policy is made.

Administrative structures and relationships are especially complex and interesting in the contemporary period. In both Britain and the United States, diplomacy in the traditional sense is managed by a foreign service which is separate from the broader civil service. At the same time, modern foreign policy questions often impinge on a wide range of government departments and agencies which are normally thought of as being domestically focused. This in turn raises important issues of co-ordination with the government for the conduct of foreign affairs, a topic of importance on both sides of the Atlantic, and one which will be considered in some detail in the course of this analysis.

There are many broad similarities, and some important contrasts, between foreign affairs organisation in Britain and the United States. The person in charge, Secretary of State or Foreign Secretary, is a senior figure in the Cabinet. In the United States, he usually has considerable foreign policy experience, and in the past has often been a major partisan political figure. In Britain, he may have foreign policy credentials, but the more important condition is status as a powerful party politician. It is clear also that political skill and forcefulness can make up for lack of formal expertise, in the sense of having effectiveness in shaping policy. While Ernest Bevin was a most influential Foreign Secretary in the period just after the Second World War, he lacked foreign affairs experience, and his trade union origins were antithetical to the aristocratic and upper-class backgrounds associated with the foreign service.

Naturally, the relationship with the Prime Minister is vital. Normally, Prime Ministers have taken a keen interest in international affairs. The striking exceptions to this, such as Stanley Baldwin, serve mainly to prove the rule. This implies the need for a good personal rapport with the Foreign Secretary if policy is to be clearly developed and smoothly implemented, and this point tends to be borne out in practical historical experience. Bevin and Clement Attlee, for example, shared a close professional relationship during the period of significant postwar British influence.[9] By contrast, two of the great recent miscalculations of British foreign policy have involved Prime Ministers who did not consult widely among either their political colleagues or civil service associates. During the period of appeasement of Hitler during the 1930s, Neville Chamberlain operated very independently of his Cabinet, including his Foreign Secretary. Anthony Eden, himself serving as Prime Minister in 1956, made the Suez invasion a very personal affair by forcing agreement from his Cabinet colleagues, in a rushed and unnatural fashion. At the time the crucial decisions were made, the foreign affairs bureaucracy was bypassed.[10] Paul Gore-Booth, who eventually became the senior career official in the Foreign Office, was posted in London at this time and recalls in his memoirs:

> It was clear from the moment I started work in October 1956 that there was something very odd and very wrong with the atmosphere in the offices and corridors. People sensed that big events were impending. They did not know what; they only knew that, to a degree unprecedented since Munich, they were not being consulted or even allowed to know.[11]

Oddly, the Conservative Party, which might be expected to be especially strict in adherence to constitutional traditions, was in office during both periods. From the viewpoint of either main party, however, there is clearly an incentive from these events of recent decades to adhere to the custom of co-operation between the two Cabinet offices chiefly concerned with foreign relations.

The Foreign Secretary is, among other things, an important source of contact and pressure between the Prime Minister and the professionals of the Foreign and Commonwealth Office. For this reason, he can play a pivotal role in moving policy in one direction or another. Diplomats, like their domestic counterparts in the civil service, stress the fundamental importance of having an assertive, forceful representative on the Cabinet. George Brown is frequently cited as a leading recent example of an especially strong Foreign Secretary. Michael Stewart held the same post during this period of Labour rule, and had considerably more familiarity with foreign affairs, but is generally regarded as having been overshadowed by his more strong-willed party colleagues. Harold Wilson notes in his memoirs that Brown was particularly happy to get the position: "George was overjoyed, and his morale rose some forty points."[12] Soon after taking over, Brown became even more vigorous in his advocacy of membership in the European Economic Community. On this subject, he was an especially assertive representative of the Foreign Office viewpoint. As one Labour politician recalls: "Brown was pro-European before, but they [the Foreign Office] made him a fanatic on the subject," adding, "An important element in Wilson's decision [to seek entry] . . . was Brown going on, and on, and on at him every day."

Below high levels of government is the professional diplomatic service itself. In Britain and the United States, a number of things differentiate domestic from foreign services, including ethos and style as well as practical professional concerns. It is common to associate diplomacy with upper-class personalities. The important ritualistic and ceremonial features of diplomacy probably make such a connection inevitable. Moreover, there is considerable empirical justification for the point that these public servants are set apart socially. In the past, an independent personal income was generally considered a prerequisite to a foreign service career, primarily because it was expected that those capable of good diplomacy would also be well-heeled, and salaries were commensurately low. Students of foreign policy practices on both sides of the Atlantic have remarked on the different characteristics of professional diplomats. Harold Seidman, in the course of a general examination of US federal government organisation, notes that: "While personal wealth is no longer a criterion, the concept of the Foreign Service as a 'gentleman's club' persists." He goes on to cite a 1966 study which discovered "remarkably similar personal backgrounds" among recruits to the foreign service.

> They came from higher income groups than their contemporaries, and included relatively few from minority races or religions. Their college education had been concentrated in the liberal arts field. Those students who specialized in business administration and management or in technical, scientific, or professional fields were not attracted to the foreign service.

Ivy League universities are heavily represented among foreign service personnel. Even more important, there has been a strong internal sentiment that such an orientation is very appropriate and desirable in the diplomatic world. George Kennan is one of the most prominent defenders of this particular sort of elitism: "I am frank to say that I cannot conceive of an effective foreign service otherwise than as a gentlemen's service."[13]

In Britain, where traditions of hierarchy and privilege run very deep, it is not surprising that historically the foreign service has been especially closely tied to the Monarchy and upper classes. It was only after the Congress of Vienna, in the first part of the nineteenth century, that a regular foreign service was set up, and the Foreign Office itself was not established until 1782. Before 1869, the money for diplomatic activities was taken out of the Civil List, the general fund for support of the Monarchy, rather than being part of the regular government budget approved by Parliament. Moreover, reflecting the complex British social structure, distinctions have existed not only between diplomats and the rest of the civil service, but also—and quite markedly—between different categories of professionals dealing with foreign affairs. Discrimination was felt especially strongly in the consular corps, which was until recently quite formally separate from the regular diplomatic fraternity, and viewed as inferior. D. C. M. Platt, in his study of the British consuls, states bluntly: "The St. James's Club in London existed for the Foreign Office and Diplomatic Service alone; it was 'known to harbour a strong prejudice against admitting members of the Consular Service.' To a diplomat, said Francis Oppenheimer, the consular official was regarded as a maid of all work. . ."[14]

Along with these very general similarities in ambience, style and relations with other parts of the government, there have also been significant differences between the two countries in the primary difficulties in foreign affairs organisation. To simplify, but also highlight contrasts, the British have had to combine various foreign services into one as part of the contraction of international influence; the Americans have been faced with a State Department increasingly overshadowed by the White House and various domestic agencies in the conduct of foreign policy.

Over the last several decades, there has been an important amalgamation of different parts of the British government dealing with foreign affairs. The reforms of 1943 were the first of several major alterations which have occurred, and were so thoroughgoing that it is customary for analysts to state that a "new" foreign service may be dated from this period. The changes were based upon a White Paper by Anthony Eden, entitled *Proposals for the Reform of the Foreign Service.* A number of administrative lines were redrawn to make diplomatic organisation more orderly and, it was hoped, more effective. There was a merger of the Foreign Office and Diplomatic Service, the Commercial Diplomatic Service, and the Consular Service into a single enlarged Foreign Office. There was also an effort to make entrance examinations more open and fair, with ambiguous results.[15]

In the middle 1960s, there was another important series of mergers, reflecting the steady retreat from empire. The Plowden Committee report on the reform of the diplomatic service was published in 1964, and the following year a new integrated service was established, composed of the previously separate Foreign, Commonwealth and Trade Commissioner services. In 1966, a new Commonwealth Office was formed by merging the Commonwealth Relations and Colonial Offices, and in 1968 this was joined with the Foreign Office to produce a completely unified foreign relations department. In 1969, another important review, the Val Duncan report, was issued, which urged further integration within the diplomatic service, modernisation of training and promotion techniques along the lines recommended in the Fulton report for the domestic service, and increased co-ordination and interchange with domestic departments.[16] A comprehensive analysis of overseas representation by the Central Policy Review Staff was completed in 1977. While perhaps more critical than some earlier reviews concerning the effectiveness of British foreign policy in broad terms, this report was in line with them in advocating greater professionalism, even more stress on export promotion, and greater interchange between the foreign and domestic services. Indeed, the "Think

Tank" report, as it was popularly called, advocated a merger of the home civil service and the diplomatic service.

In the United States, a constant theme of foreign policy reformers has been the cumbersome and ineffective qualities of State Department bureaucracy. Where the British have focused on the effort to contract and unify a diverse and farflung collection of foreign services, the Americans have been confronted with the reverse situation of adjusting to a significantly expanded international role. The interesting question still occurs, however, of why the Foreign Office in Britain has generally avoided the criticisms levelled at, and actual weaknesses of, the American State Department. Aside from the requirements of periodic formal pronouncements about the need for a strong State Department occupying a central position in the conduct of foreign policy, recent Presidents have neither concerned themselves with practical aspects of strengthening its organisation nor taken steps to reverse the flow of power in other directions. Presidents Roosevelt, Kennedy and Nixon have all complained openly about the lack of satisfactory performance by State. Kennedy's remark that the department was a "bowl of jelly" has been echoed in less colourful statements by other Chief Executives. A range of government and private commissions on foreign policy organisation have addressed the problem, without so far having a significant impact on the situation. With increasing frequency, Presidents have turned to special personal assistants for the co-ordination and actual formation of foreign policy. Two recent strong Secretaries of State, John Foster Dulles and Henry Kissinger, have played a very personal sort of diplomacy, ignoring organisational problems and—in the former case—willingly sacrificing subordinates to the pressures of domestic politics.[17]

Several factors come immediately to mind when considering the position of the State Department and the apparent lack of comparable problems in Britain. First, American foreign policy officials have been much more vulnerable to the vicissitudes of domestic policies. It is not just that the United States is a more democratic country. The enormous psychological adjustments required by American involvement in a range of "entangling alliances" after the Second World War, and the traumatic domestic reaction to the development of the Cold War—especially the Communist victory in China—had a very important impact on the public mood within the United States. Long-term damage was done to State Department morale and initiative by the domestic political attacks and criticism of the 1940s and early 1950s. There has been no comparable involvement of British foreign policy agencies in domestic controversy.

Second, one of the most interesting, and historically significant, developments in the conduct of American foreign policy has been the close personal rapport between three particular Presidents and their Special Assistants for National Security Affairs. The personalities involved have varied considerably, but there has been the constant factor of excellent working partnerships between Kennedy and McGeorge Bundy, Johnson and Walt Rostow, and Nixon and Henry Kissinger. This series of coincidences of personality, which contains rich material for analysis by political scientists and others concerned with foreign affairs, has had the practical result of moving sharply the centre of action in important foreign policy matters from the State Department to the White House. Even in the Kennedy Administration, where Bundy served very much as a facilitator of communication between the President and other sectors of the government, generally presenting the case for different policies rather than guiding decisions in a particular direction, the National Security Council was the vital centre of decision-making.[18] Again, the situation contrasts with Britain. In recent years, the British Cabinet Office has become increasingly important in foreign policy, especially in terms of co-ordinating the wide range of domestic departments with significant interests in European Economic Community matters. However, there has been nothing comparable to the dramatic overshadowing of the State Department by the National Security Council.

In British foreign policy, as in domestic policy, the committee system governs decision-making and co-ordinates implementation. To be sure, interdepartmental committees have proliferated widely in Washington since the Second World War as a source of communication on foreign policy matters. Nevertheless, they are neither so strongly rooted nor as flexible as in Britain. The principal British Cabinet Committee concerned with foreign affairs is the Defence and Overseas Policy Committee. It is a successor to the Defence Committee established after the war, which was in turn based upon the old Committee of Imperial Defence, set up before the First World War. In the United States, no strong need to establish a formal top-level committee to co-ordinate foreign affairs in broad terms was felt until after the Second World War, when the National Security Council was established. In part, this contrast reflects different customs and traditions concerning use of government committees. It also underlines the much more recent beginning of American involvement in a substantial foreign affairs role.[19]

The lack of a comparable committee tradition in the United States, and the concomitant weaker habit of consultation across departmental lines, has made co-ordination much more difficult and unreliable, and draws attention to the need for a central mechanism to help establish and maintain links. Weakness of the State Department, the natural co-ordinating agency, has rendered it unable to provide this service. The White House has filled the breach not primarily by providing improved co-ordination, but rather through centralisation of power concerning policy areas of particular concern to the President. In recent years, hostility toward the State Department has accentuated the trend. Nixon and Kissinger assumed office with a strong dislike and suspicion of State Department bureaucracy. After becoming Secretary of State, Kissinger's many activities and interests did not include concern with the administrative organisation of his department. In the United States, where the scale of government is much larger than in Britain and traditions of informal co-ordination not nearly so strong, it is necessary to address very explicitly the problem of communication within government. So far, attention to this subject at the highest levels has been decidedly sporadic.[20]

Another factor which sharply differentiates the two national situations is the role of the Treasury in Britain. Though in some ways not as powerful as in the past, this department remains enormously important. It combines functions which in the United States are distributed among the Treasury Department, the Office of Management and Budget, and other parts of the executive branch. Until the separate Civil Service Department was created in 1968, the Treasury managed personnel practices and rules as well. It therefore has played an especially prominent and wideranging role, which has no direct parallel in the American system. Once again, the position of the Treasury has been significant for administration across the board, but also for the more specific area of the conduct of foreign policy.

It is the Treasury which reviews spending plans of various departments, and bargains and compromises with other civil servants in the process of working out final annual government expenditures. The actual level of budgets of the Foreign and Commonwealth Office is not an item of major importance. As in the US, diplomacy formally and narrowly conceived is a relatively inexpensive activity. However, a range of other areas of government, including but not limited to defence, are directly and indirectly of significance to foreign affairs. In this sense, there has been a continuing conflict between the Treasury and other parts of the bureaucracy. It is fair to say that for most of the period since the Second World War, the Foreign Office and Defence Ministry have been consistently straining against Treasury efforts to rein in the total overseas involvements of Britain. Defence and diplomatic officials have been concerned to maintain current commitments and loyalty to earlier ambitions; Treasury representatives have been anxious to restrict the costly drain of these activities.[21]

This situation has had an important impact on the conduct of foreign policy and the components of intragovernmental conflict in the postwar period. First, the antagonism involving the Treasury has tended to mute conflicts between other departments. The fact that, in the words of one prominent observer of British foreign policy, ". . . the Treasury is the enemy of all civil servants", tends to create alliances of convenience among a range of officials to strengthen their position against Treasury administrators. The desire to defend one another for mutual advantage against the guardians of the budget means that, in many ways, the most significant cleavage in British administration is the one between the Treasury and other departments. In consequence, conflicts which have been of some importance in the US, such as those between the State and Defense Departments, or State and the White House, have been considerably less significant in Britain.

Second, the Treasury's control over finance, combined with the shrinking international economic position of Britain since the Second World War, means that the department has played a central part in the definition of specific limits and parameters of policy. Major British defence policy reviews and shifts have been carried out largely as a result of Treasury urging. Devaluation of the pound was delayed until 1967 partly because of Treasury resistance. Treasury opposition to entry into the Common Market did not prevent a reversal of policy in 1961 to favour entry, but did make a difference in the style and means by which the nation approached negotiation.

Third, and related to this point, tensions between the Foreign Office and the Treasury concerning the wisdom of maintaining old international defence obligations, and taking on new economic ones in Europe, has meant that the former department is not generally recognised as an unbiased, neutral arbiter within the government on foreign policy questions. The Treasury negotiates with, polices and reviews other parts of the bureaucracy. Its function precludes a neutral role, or rather involves continual negotiation, adversary proceedings, and conciliation among a large array of departments, constantly guided by the desire to restrict expenditures to a minimal level consistent with sensible public policy. The Foreign Office, in a position much different from that of financial monitor, might be expected to perform as primary co-ordinator in foreign relations, an increasingly complex and significant task in the age of multilateral diplomacy. In fact, this has not happened, and the Foreign Office's position of general advocacy of international involvements would tend to remove the flexibility and ambiguity of position useful to an agency seeking to draw others together.

Other considerations are also important here, including the point that Prime Ministers since the Second World War have been uniformly leaders with a keen interest in foreign affairs. It is natural therefore that the main staff agency for the head of government should assume a stronger role in this field, and creditable that this has been done comparatively smoothly. In addition, the Foreign Office is generally viewed as lacking the technical skill and sophistication necessary for complex multilateral diplomacy, including the especially complicated issues attending European Economic Community membership. Nevertheless, while the department has not had a decisive role, it has been able to maintain influence on foreign policy generally, without sharp breaks with the Prime Minister and Cabinet Office. As one would expect from different structural and cultural traditions, the British have confronted problems of organisation and expertise in foreign affairs similar to those in the US, but have responded generally by maintaining fluidity and avoiding creation of dominant power centres. Conflicts have been present, but more muted; and they have been solved, but in undramatic fashion. This point may be further developed through specific reference to the organisational arrangements involved.

REFORMS AND ADJUSTMENTS

Discussion so far has focused primarily on the differences between Britain and the US, in the structures for foreign affairs decision-making and administration, and the pressures which bear upon them. The point should also be made that there are important similarities in current major issues of foreign policy organisation. While the policy traditions, and concrete organisations, of major nations may differ, contemporary concerns in many ways appear to be very much alike.

The growth in significance of multilateral diplomacy, normally defined as comparatively technical sorts of relations, has focused attention on the interplay and arrangements among various government departments, including those concerned principally with domestic policy. Such subjects as military and arms control policy have created problems of policy co-ordination for a number of years. In the present period, important concerns include trade and investment, international monetary matters, food and other commodity shortages, and energy, environmental and other scientific and technological issues. To be sure, economic relations among nations have always been significant, and doubtless during any period in history foreign policy officials have been impressed by the complexity of their occupations. The main point is that economic questions have recently assumed much greater political importance.

Students of foreign policy have frequently made this point in recent years. Two might be cited for their observations concerning the countries here under discussion. David Vital, in examining Britain's current international position, states: ". . . increasingly in the modern period, the traditional and *a priori* distinction between foreign and domestic affairs has been breaking down in Britain—as elsewhere. Policy in one field will be justified in terms of the other in a way which would have struck nineteenth century foreign ministers as odd, even unseemly."[22] Destler, considering problems of foreign policy organisation in the US, takes the same view: "Precision is impossible . . . in distinguishing 'foreign' from other types of national policy. International issues are becoming more and more intertwined with a range of domestic policy interests. . ."[23]

There have been both similarities and contrasts between British and American proposals for improvement in the conduct of foreign relations. A steady theme in a large number of government and privately sponsored reports on the subject in the US has been the search for devices to strengthen the State Department, or at least define more clearly its relationship to the rest of the government. Nevertheless, the fact that this has been a subject of concern for a number of years does not mean that we are closer to a solution. William Bacchus, a specialist on the subject and a staff member of the Murphy Commission, the latest in the series of formal government efforts to address the situation, has observed along this line: "Proposals and recommendations have come from many individuals, and from numerous official and quasi-official bodies, but there has been a general failure to find lasting solutions. In view of an increasingly evident need for improvement, however, these failures have served only to generate still other reform programs."[24] There has been no comparable emphasis in Britain, where the Foreign and

Commonwealth Office has been able to change its composition and relationship with the Cabinet Office and other departments, while avoiding a general loss of influence and position.

At the same time, in both countries there has been growing concern to foster closer integration of domestic and foreign policy agencies, and to provide diplomatic personnel with greater sophistication and skill in handling technical subjects. This in turn has led to proposals for seconding people, at least on a temporary basis, between domestic and foreign services. Such interchange in practice has been restricted by a number of predictable stumbling-blocks, including problems of transition between different grading and salary structures, lack of available slots which would provide significant experience, and the possibility of having promotion prospects damaged as a result of spending time in an agency formally unrelated to a conventional career ladder.

In the United States, one of the most important reform efforts of recent years occurred early in the Nixon Administration, thanks primarily to the initiative of Deputy Under-Secretary of State William Macomber. Secretary of State William Rogers reflected his predecessors in having a general lack of concern with organisational matters. His deputy, Elliot Richardson, however, was keenly interested in the subject, and encouraged an atmosphere conducive to reform. A number of task forces were established to address management problems, under the general direction of Macomber, and their draft reports were completed by mid-1970. Ambitious changes in foreign service career patterns were advocated. Unfortunately for the reformers, however, comparatively little concrete implementation occurred.

> The unification of the personnel systems began with the announcement of the creation of a Foreign Affairs Specialist Corps (FAS), into which some Foreign Service Staff Officers (FSSOs), Reserve Officers (FSRs), and a limited number of FSOs and Civil Servants in State were to be encouraged to transfer. . . However, this unification was stymied by legal action initiated on the grounds that civil service employees would lose some protection by becoming members of the Foreign Service system.[25]

Other problems arose to frustrate the proposed reforms. Efforts to foster non-examination recruitment "have foundered because of financial and numerical restrictions". It was unfortunate for the Macomber initiative that the State Department at this time was undergoing a substantial attrition in total number of foreign service officers, which limited severely the possibilities for imaginative movements of personnel. More generally, there clearly was resistance to far-reaching reform on the part of significant numbers of foreign policy professionals. As one of the Macomber reports put it:

> Psychologically, the Foreign Service officer is a permanent transient; his home is his profession . . . These conditions of the profession engender a clan mentality, a sense of detachment from the physical environment of the moment and from the community of ordinary Americans as a whole. Clannishness can result in a "don't rock the boat" attitude as well as a career protectiveness against outsiders and new ideas.[26]

In Britain, where social structures are more complex and more differentiated, there has been even stronger resistance to any close integration of domestic and foreign services. At the same time, problems of Britain's international position have provided an especially great incentive to take action toward reform. The Plowden Commission report of 1964 was concerned with the problems of integrating various diplomatic and overseas services. With publication of the Val Duncan report in 1969, other concerns were given attention as well, including abolition of the old civil service "class" ranks and substituting a more systematic and contemporary series of formal grades.[27]

The Val Duncan report also discussed economic and commercial matters in some detail, an emphasis which is not surprising in view of Britain's gradual but steady loss of position among the economies of the world. The report stressed ". . . the clear precedence that belongs to the commercial objective in the day-to-day conduct of Britain's relations with other countries. There are other aims of policy, some of them of high importance, but they cannot be effectively pursued if the balance of payments is not put right." Following this expression of concern, it was noted in the report that overseas relations should be more sharply divided into two broad categories. The priority area was to be ". . . advanced industrial countries with which we are likely to be increasingly involved to the point where none of us will be able to conduct our domestic policies efficiently without constant reference to each other". This category consisted of Western Europe, North America, and a few other advanced industrial nations such as Australia and Japan. It was to be ". . . the Area of Concentration of British diplomacy". There was also stress on devoting increased attention to furthering British commercial interests, and especially those of export firms.[28]

Different practical tools have been employed in the attempt to modernise and increase the efficiency and responsiveness of the British diplomatic service. One has been the Civil Service Staff College, first established as the Centre for Administrative Studies in Regents Park in London in 1963. Following the Fulton report's appearance, it was expanded and made more substantial, and a new main facility was set up at Sunningdale.[29] Additionally, as with American reform efforts, there has been an attempt to promote greater integration of domestic and foreign services. The Val Duncan report noted that the need for overseas postings justified a separate diplomatic service, but added that ". . . while a distinct Diplomatic Service should be maintained, the degree of separateness should be as little as possible".[30]

Again, as in the United States, reforms have been restricted by various barriers. It has been difficult to free many civil servants for the technical training available at the College, and terms of instruction have generally been brief. There has been considerable resistance to closer integration of the two services. This subject has generally been treated gingerly by formal bodies charged with reviewing and proposing changes in administration, doubtless because it touches on traditional social divisions within the government service. Samuel Brittan, a perceptive and candid journalistic analyst, has addressed this subject directly in his important study of the Treasury, *Steering the Economy:*

> Fulton indeed missed one obvious reform, which would probably make more practical difference than the abolition of classes. This would be to unify the Home and Overseas Civil Services. The case for unification is particularly strong now that the commercial and economic aspects of diplomatic work are so heavily emphasised. Under present arrangements these tasks are bound to seem chores which few diplomats can carry out with first-hand knowledge. Equally, officials in home departments too often have to speculate, with no real background understanding, about the overseas implications of British policies. Such a unification would widen the horizon of both branches and would have a genuine effect on *social* class barriers in the one area of Whitehall where they still exist. The very ferocity with which the proposal is so often resisted shows how near the bone it reaches.[31]

Another outside critic of the *status quo* responds to the issue by noting that ". . . a lot of unmentionable things" are involved, and that diplomats resist integration by arguing that domestic civil servants are unwilling to consider overseas work because ". . . you get great hairy spiders in your bathroom".

Certainly members of the foreign service emphasise the alleged reluctance of their domestic counterparts to undertake the rigours of being posted elsewhere in the world. To quote one who is typical of many: "I wouldn't see very much more scope for integration because the basic difference between out two services is that our service is supposed to go anywhere . . . we aren't willing to give nice posts to people who aren't willing to take the nasty ones."

If diplomats consider themselves a breed apart from the rest of the professional civil service, their domestic colleagues also stress differences. From this perspective, the gap is said to result, as noted earlier, from the alleged lack of administrative and technical skill among people in the overseas service. This point often blends with the related one that diplomats lack bureaucratic finesse. Then too, the Foreign Office is considered a centre of commitment. To quote several domestic civil servants: "I think it is sensible [to have the Cabinet Office co-ordinate European affairs]. For many years, the ministries involved were too suspicious of the Foreign Office to comfortably sit on committees under their chairmanship." Concerning diplomats' approach to international affairs generally, he adds: "We in the Treasury felt the Foreign Office were too easily taken in by their own propaganda, without regard to cost . . . In truth, they never had as good people as we had. We could always beat them at it." Another civil servant complained that diplomats have no experience in spending money and "don't know how to work the Whitehall machine . . .".

In summary, efforts to reform dramatically the relationship between foreign and domestic policy administration, and the composition and background of the diplomatic service, have not been very successful in Britain, just as they have not in the United States. Along with a range of practical stumbling-blocks, there have also been important and subtle social distinctions involved. This has not only discouraged reform efforts, it has also encouraged advertising rather minor changes as being much more significant than the facts justified. The Val Duncan report's division of the world into two general diplomatic areas, presented with stress on its novelty, actually reflected long-standing informal practice in British foreign policy. To quote one foreign service official: "There has always been an emphasis on the

States and Europe. A tour of the States is important for someone going right to the top of the service. "

Nevertheless, if there has been no decisive reform of the administration of British foreign policy, there has been a steady and relatively smooth adjustment to a significantly altered international system. The Foreign Office has not been dominant, but neither has it been submerged. It should be noted that the department has been generally successful in placing representatives at the head of important missions overseas. European entry was promoted early by the Foreign Office, which recognised that region as an area of opportunity for British diplomacy. Different services and offices dealing with overseas matters have been combined, again with an absence of crisis and sharp internal differences. The general British approach to public policy has been present in the more specific realm of foreign affairs, enabling the nation to adjust to changes in many ways more difficult than those faced by the US, without parallel internal divisions and ruptures in policy organisation.

3 Military and Strategic Change

Military power is an important indicator of international political influence. Britain ended the Second World War as one of the three main Allied nations not only because of successful resistance against German attack, but also because of the substantial military strength which made possible both defence and participation in a significant way in the campaigns against the Axis. Since the war, British decline has involved shrinkage and contraction of military capacity. In turn, military reductions have been a direct reflection of the serious economic problems besetting the nation. The base upon which foreign policy is made was becoming weaker, with decisive implications for the military as well as other elements of foreign policy.

The end of the Second World War brought changes in military policy, but these reflected the pressures of a changed international environment rather than a positive and assertive British definition of a new role and position. Faced with serious domestic and international economic problems, political difficulties resulting from enforced neglect of social reforms at home, and committed anyway more to internal affairs than international influence, the Labour government pressed ahead with postwar demobilisation. As in the United States, the period 1945–8 was something of a hiatus, following the defeat of the Axis and before the Cold War with the Soviet Union had really settled over Europe. Moreover, the willingness of the Americans to take up burdens in Germany and the Mediterranean facilitated British retreat.

The British did give important priority to development of atomic weapons capabilities. Aside from the inherent difficulties of building this type of bomb, British determination is reflected in the willingness of the nation to press ahead with development despite the political barriers as well as technical complications. During the Second World War, President Roosevelt and Prime Minister Churchill had agreed to collaborate closely on atomic energy matters; later, Canada was included in this understanding. With the end of the war, however, the Americans experienced a change of heart; or, perhaps more accurately, secret understandings reached by the dead President became known more broadly, and in Congress and elsewhere there was a reaction of distrust concerning sharing vital information with foreign countries, even close allies. This entire subject is discussed and analysed in detail in Chapter 5; for now, the important point is that in the late summer of 1946 the McMahon Act was passed and became law. This legislation prohibited sharing atomic information with any foreign country, including Britain. In response, the British decided to press ahead with their own atomic bomb, even while maintaining the basic diplomatic concord with the Americans.

On the conventional plane, the British drastically cut back total forces. There was still a range of commitments around the globe after the war. Forces were engaged in conflicts in some of these, notably Palestine, Greece and Malaya. Nevertheless, there was an overall reduction in military manpower from over 2 million in 1946 to 1.3 million in early 1947.[1]

Soon after this Britain, along with the Atlantic area nations, was caught up in the atmosphere of the emerging Cold War conflict with the Soviet Union. Conventional forces were expanded in response to this general shift in the climate of foreign relations, and to the specific challenge represented by the Korean War. Additionally, rising tensions contributed to more co-operative relations with the United States in the atomic field. In 1947, the US was confronted with serious ore shortages in uranium, hampering nuclear weapon manufacture. This pressure led to a new Anglo-American agreement, and the US received uranium from Congo mines. In return, although the McMahon Act was not changed, the British were relieved of wartime restrictions on commercial and industrial use of atomic energy, and received some technical information on the American programme. It was to be a decade, however, before the McMahon law was reformed to permit general sharing of information with Britain.[2]

The Korean War had a great impact on Europe. As at other times since, NATO nations felt that a crisis elsewhere in the world was directed at their region. As Richard Rosecrance has observed:

With large numbers of American troops pinned down in the Far Eastern "quagmire", Europe was all the more vulnerable. Korea might be the necessary diversion for an attack on Europe. Very little attention seems to have been paid at the time to the fact that Secretary Acheson, in extending the US defense perimeter in January, 1950, to include Japan, had omitted the defense of Korea.[3]

There was also a substantial British rearmament programme. During the early part of Korean hostilities, the Attlee government announced a greatly enlarged defence effort, totalling £3400 million over three years. This was boosted further soon thereafter to a total of £4700 million. Such a programme in the best of foreseeable circumstances would have imposed a serious burden on the British economy. In the event, balance-of-payments deficits and raw materials shortages compelled the Conservative government which took office in 1951 to retrench. The rearmament programme was extended from three years to four. Continuing economic problems dragged it further behind schedule. Nevertheless, there was a significant expansion of the defence establishment. Manpower levels, for example, rose from 690,000 in 1950 to a peak of 875,000 in 1952. Thereafter, there was a fairly steady decline—to a total of 700,000 in 1957, and 425,000 in 1962.[4]

This peak and then decline in military forces reflected the strictures of economic problems, but also indicated that Britain and the United States were moving towards the "New Look" which emphasised nuclear weapons as the basic component of the defence structure. The Eisenhower Administration, strongly concerned with the dangers of inflation, put economic considerations above military, and by doing so cut four billion dollars from defence spending in 1954. In a similar manner, the Conservative governments of the same period in Britain were able to hold the line on defence spending, and achieve an actual reduction when the effects of inflation are taken into account. British defence budgets did not begin to rise again in real terms until 1960.[5]

The British decision to develop a nuclear force was voluntary in the context of the NATO Alliance. The Alliance did not formerly allocate a strategic atomic role to the British. Rather, the United States was to fulfill this function. The emphasis for European NATO partners was on ground and tactical air capabilities. Nevertheless, in the early 1950s the British proceeded not only with the development of the bomb, but also with a strategic air force to deliver it. It was suggested in defence debates in 1953 that the government might develop this capacity. The policy was made explicit in the Defence White Paper of 1954:

> The primary deterrent, however, remains the atomic bomb and the ability of the highly organised and trained United States strategic air power to use it. From our past experience and current knowledge

we have a significant contribution to make both to the technical and to the tactical development of strategic air power. We intend as soon as possible to build up in the Royal Air Force a force of modern bombers capable of using the atomic weapon to the fullest effect.[6]

Naturally, a significant new military effort was required to develop a separate national strategic capability. Bomber Command, a basic part of the military structure during the Second World War, was revitalised. A substantial buildup of bomber forces continued during the period 1955–7. Principal reliance was placed on the "V" series of bombers, which included the Valiant, Victor and Vulcan. Bombers were the basic element in the programme to develop a strategic delivery capability for atomic weapons. American emphasis on the Strategic Air Command was complementary and encouraged the British in this direction.[7]

Looking to the future, British planners realised that the bomber force which provided the strategic backbone of the mid-1950s would be obsolete relatively soon. In consequence, development of the Blue Streak missile was begun in the early 1950s. This was designed to be a liquid-fuel missile, to be launched from underground sites, with a range of between two thousand and twenty-five hundred miles. It would not have the reach of the new intercontinental ballistic missiles being developed in the United States and, presumably, the Soviet Union. It would, however, surpass existing intermediate range missiles, such as the Thor and Jupiter. Therefore, the British would be able to argue that they were making a contribution to the strategic arsenal of the West.[8]

During the same period, work was begun on a second missile, Blue Steel. It was designed to be launched from under the wings of bombers, at a distance of approximately one hundred miles from the target. It was similar to the more sophisticated and advanced American Skybolt missile, and would serve the role of buying time during the development of Blue Streak. As William Snyder puts it in his comprehensive study of British defence policy since the Second World War: "Blue Steel was expected to prolong the period of service of the V-bombers already in use by reducing their vulnerability to air defences in the period immediately prior to the availability of the Blue Streak."[9]

British strategic developments in the 1950s are revealing concerning the more general international position of the nation. Into the second half of the decade, it was possible and reasonable for policy-makers to assume that there were no significant problems standing in the way of an influential position, one which would be at least roughly comparable to that of the United States or the Soviet Union. It was decided to go ahead with a British hydrogen bomb in 1954, a clear sign of a desire to stay on the same nuclear road being travelled by the two new superpowers. If it had been clear as early as the Second World War that the British lacked the enormous technological structure the Americans could muster, the quality of British scientific research rightly commanded respect. If the British had to search for ways to prolong the life and extend the range of ageing bombers, that hardly meant there was no strategic role left.[10]

RATIONALES FOR POLICY

The British decision to develop nuclear weapons has frequently been subjected to criticism, not only from abroad but also at home, by observers who believe represents national overreaching and unwillingness to accept the reduced circumstances of the postwar period. The British insisted on trying to maintain great-power status during a time of gradual but steady economic decline. The criticism of this situation customarily has put great stress on lack of foresight revealed in trying to develop a strategic capability which the economy could not afford at an effective level. Such discussions, at least to some extent, blend with separate but related consideration of the more general problem of nuclear proliferation. Often, criticism combines accusations that British policy has contributed to the spread of nuclear weapons and has resulted in a force lacking sufficient power to be influential. In effect, Britain is chided for pursuing dangerous policies, yet achieving a position which still leaves the nation dwarfed by the two superpowers.[11]

Actually, it is not at all surprising that the British decided to move ahead with the atomic force, nor is the step really difficult to defend on strategic or more practical political grounds. The nation was accustomed to a diverse array of international involvements, and until the mid-1950s was able to handle them skilfully and with comparative ease. History aside, it remained a basic reality that Britain was one of the very few nations possessing the scientific and technical capacity to manufacture the atomic bomb. If the British had decided against going ahead with the weapon, it would have been very perplexing, amounting to abandonment of a great-power position which had always been conveted. As Rosecrance has put it:

The prestige deriving from membership [in the nuclear club] was unquestioned; the feat entailed in joining unchallenged. To decide in 1945–6 to make bombs required enormous scientific power, and no little political prowess and presumption. Such decisions were reserved to the major actors of the international stage. The merits of nuclear status were unequivocal; the disadvantages almost non-existent. It was not surprising that Britain opted for bombs; it would have been remarkable if she had not done so.[12]

The British saw two basic justifications for the development of their own atomic force. First, it would provide for defence of the nation at a time when American commitment to Europe was uncertain. The shape of the postwar international system was still emerging when the British made the decision to develop the bomb. The US might become formally committed to the defence of Europe, but also had a long history and powerful tradition of isolationism. Uncertainty concerning American willingness to defend Europe was a strong incentive to take steps to ensure a strong British position. Second, the British wished to gain influence with the United States and the other significant powers and lesser nations of the world. Atomic weapons provided the necessary status for doing so, and moreover continued to be useful even while the overall position of the nation declined. During the first decade after the Second World War, possession of the bomb reinforced the image of Britain as a great power on a par with the United States and the Soviet Union. Later, after it was clear that the British were no longer on the same level with the two nuclear giants, such weapons were still useful to maintenance of status as a middle power. Below the positions of the superpowers, the British—like the French—realised that nuclear weapons could be used to differentiate their nation from almost all the others in the world.[13]

Both justifications for atomic weapons draw attention to the pivotal position of Britain in the Atlantic area during the period just after the war, and the importance of a strong military posture to that role. Britain was linked to both Europe and the US, but psychologically separated from each. By developing an independent deterrent, it would be possible to facilitate relations between both sides of the Atlantic by blurring differences which separated them. The Europeans would be reassured that a nation within their region had a nuclear capacity; the Americans would have a further incentive to heed British advice. Alliance relations would be complicated usefully in the sense that there would not be a totally stark contrast between a nuclear-armed US and a conventionally armed Western Europe.

In summary, the British, in contrast to what came later in the decade, moved through the first half of the 1950s in a comparatively strong military position. Economic conditions imposed restraints upon defence capabilities, but these were partial rather than decisive. The British had forces to commit to Europe, manned various positions throughout the Commonwealth, and developed a nuclear capacity. One important reason why they did not choose between Commonwealth, European and nuclear-strategic dimensions during this period is that they had the ability to operate within all three. The British rather naturally played a role in the great-power conferences of the period, notably the 1954 Geneva discussions which brought an end to the Indochina war. Britain had American attention, leverage in Europe, and many other international involvements. Far from being overcome by postwar developments, the British military was dealing effectively with several local wars, including conflicts in Cyprus and Palestine, and the Mau Mau insurgency in Kenya.

This situation was sharply reversed by later events, illustrated most dramatically by the Suez fiasco of 1956. Suez may have of itself seriously damaged Britain's political image and influence around the world. More fundamentally, the way in which the crisis was worked out showed that Britain was considerably weaker than the nation's leaders, and others, had believed. Suez also clarified incipient differences at home within the domestic polity concerning the proper role of the nation internationally. Both domestically and internationally, the reverberations from Suez were very severe, and justify viewing the event as a turning point in the thrust and tone of British foreign policy since the Second World War.

The crisis was precipitated by Egyptian President Nasser's seizure of the Suez Canal, which had been under the control of an international company following British withdrawal from the former colony. Nasser's act in turn led to a secret Israeli–French–British plan for an invasion to retake the canal and depose the Nasser government as well. In late October 1956, the sudden offensive began. The British and French launched an attack against Egypt to damage war-making capability and reoccupy the Canal as Israeli military units moved across the Gaza Strip and Sinai Peninsula. However, with unexpected abruptness the attack was brought to a halt. This was the result not of Arab efforts, but rather of American pressure. President Eisenhower and Secretary of State John Foster Dulles simply and directly threatened to cease providing backing for British loans and the always fragile pound in international money markets. The British had no margin for manoeuvre. With credit suspended, the nation would have been placed in very serious economic straits. Presented with intolerable pressure, which was made all the more painful because it was so easily imposed, the British relented, reversed policy and brought their French and Israeli allies along with them.

Domestic political reactions in Britain occurred immediately. On the elite level, debate in Parliament was heated and acrimonious. Early in 1957, Prime Minister Eden resigned, ostensibly for health reasons, but the basic cause of his departure was Suez and his central involvement in the invasion scheme. More generally, both the left and right of the political spectrum were agitated by the affair. The nation had been revealed to be considerably more dependent than many people had believed. In specific terms, different political viewpoints could find reason for great concern in the way the crisis was handled. Those on the left were shocked that such a move, reminiscent of old-fashioned great-power military diplomacy, had been attempted. Those on the right were bitter and frustrated that the operation had not been pressed through to success. Failure was not enough for the left; a gesture was insufficient to satisfy the right. Parliamentary debate reflected more general concern through the nation. Trafalgar Square witnessed angry demonstrations on the part of those who believed British imperialism was threatening to revive.

The scale of the Suez failure draws attention to the reasons why the British government of the time believed it could be successfully carried through. In reality, the adventure was not undertaken by the British government at all in the sense normally understood. Rather, Eden and a very small circle of confidants pushed through the decision. As noted earlier, customary consultation within the government and civil service was not undertaken. Instead of being a failure of conventional channels for intragovernment consultation and policy formulation, Suez represents a result of shortcircuiting and going around existing structures and practices. Ironically, Eden, who suffered personally from Chamberlain's desire to run a personal foreign policy and exclude colleagues from decisions, nevertheless followed a similar course. Basically, and adding further to the irony of the situation, he appears to have been reacting against his own diplomatic experience as Foreign Secretary during the period just before the Second World War. In Eden's mind, Nasser was identified as another Hitler, and acquiescence to him would involve an appeasement as dangerous as that pursued by the Chamberlain government before the war. Eden tried to learn from experience, but even the most sympathetic interpretation must conclude that only a partial lesson was obtained. Chamberlain's misjudgement of Hitler was clearly understood; the value and importance of consultation on policy was not.

Eden's greatest error was the miscalculation about the American response. The explanation appears to be that there was an assumption that NATO allies, confronted with a *fait accompli* and an operation in progress, would have no choice but to go along with it. Relations between the United States and Egypt had become progressively more strained, reaching a culmination of sorts in the cancellation of American aid for the Aswan Dam project. In reaction, Nasser had turned to the Soviet Union. Doubtless it was anticipated that the US, already at odds with Egypt, would go along because the cause of anti-Communism was joined with the necessity for Alliance unity.

In fact, Eisenhower and Dulles were unmoved by these considerations in the face of others which Eden ignored. Aside from fear of involvement in a continuing war, there was the related point that the United States at the time was in the concluding days of the 1956 Presidential campaign. It would hardly have been wise for a President who stressed that he had kept the peace to allow his nation to become drawn, even indirectly, into an armed conflict in the Middle East. Again, the fact that Eden miscalculated so seriously concerning the American response reflects the hurried and secretive manner in which policy was made.[14]

THE COURSE OF POLICY

Following Suez, there was a change of government, and a drastic drop in the prestige and international position of Britain. To be sure, British power would continue to be deployed, generally with success, in small-scale conflicts in different corners of the globe. At the same time, it was no longer possible to pretend that room for manoeuvre and engagement was as open as it had been during previous decades. Far from being a great power, Britain had been revealed to be extremely weak, vulnerable to American pressure which could be easily imposed. Economic pressures had been growing for a long time, but were by then so severe that they could no longer be ignored in the definition of defence policy and commitments.

At the same time, there was no major change in military posture, or in the forces and commitments with Britain maintained. Rather, there was a general and across-the-board reduction in military spending.

Britain had suffered a defeat, but this did not have the effect of bringing about major policy adjustments. Suez occurred in the context of a continuing study of the British defence effort, which led to a shrinkage of budget and capabilities, combined with maintenance of the various conventional and nuclear dimensions of national military policy. Even before the Suez operation was planned, Eden and his advisers had determined that the nation would have to reduce its military burdens. After the Suez failure, there was continued implementation of these plans without major change. The British attitude is often contrasted with the French. France was also defeated at Suez, but with different consequences. It was a nation which had been beset with domestic and international difficulties for a number of years. Defeated in the Second World War, groping for a viable national government and identity, it was not regarded at home or abroad as a great power. Without the burden of struggling to maintain a position comparable to those of the US and the Soviet Union, the French were provided with more freedom to undertake policy innovations. They could explore new possibilities, and did so effectively by abandoning costly overseas holdings and developing their own nuclear force. [15]

In 1956, Eden had ordered a general paper to be prepared evaluating Britain's international position and making recommendations for the future. Economic pressures provided a strong incentive to address this subject, especially since American aid was drawing to a close. Given these kinds of considerations, it was inevitable that major emphasis would be on methods for cutting costs while retaining effectiveness. This activity provided a prelude to the significant White Paper of 1957, prepared under the direction of Minister of Defence Duncan Sandys. It was decided to give primary emphasis in British defence to the nuclear deterrent, at the expense of conventional forces. In the past, Britain had tried to have substantial capabilities in both areas. In the future, one would receive clear priority. A number of factors underlay this decision. First, an enormous amount of money had already been invested in weapons programmes. The hydrogen bomb was emerging, and development of the V-bombers had been finished. Missile development was also well under way. Future cost problems were not yet visible in 1957; past investment was a strong incentive to continue along the nuclear road. Second, in terms of doctrine, the British were strongly persuaded that nuclear weapons could perform a variety of important tasks. They were a source of prestige, placing the nation in the ranks of the great powers. They also could be used to deter both nuclear and conventional conflicts. Possession of them, it was argued, would make any opponent think twice. In this sense, the New Look still maintained a strong hold on British defence thinking. Third, they were expensive, but need not be enormously so. Because they were so powerful and destructive, it was argued that comparatively few would still provide great diplomatic impact and influence. Fourth, savings could be made by cutting conventional forces. Because there was no totally strict division made between conventional and nuclear situations, one type of force could be reduced without great anxiety. The British wanted to abolish conscription, which could not be done if ground force levels were maintained. Conscription in peacetime had not existed since 1815. It was not a policy with which the British felt comfortable, and the Sandys approach therefore persuasively married strategic argument with domestic political considerations.[16]

Nevertheless, the Sandys changes were less decisive in reality than the formal outline implies. Expenditures were cut and ceilings imposed, but there was a serious asymmetry in policy because actual commitments were not reduced. The British were determined to retain ground forces in Europe. In addition, they did not abandon the multiplicity of conventional commitments around the globe. The enormous British empire was giving way to a series of independent nations; but granting of independence often meant that the British stayed on, to honour military defence obligations which continued in force. The very process of cutting back on conventional forces, as long as these ties were maintained, meant that costs would rise. There was pressing need to increase airlift capabilities to compensate for reduction of forces already in position. In addition, ending conscription meant that service had to be more attractive and lucrative.[17]

The fact that force reductions were not balanced by contraction of obligations meant that there were constant pressures on policy and strains on the military budget. Into the 1960s, the British found themselves confronted with the need to make extra and unexpected expenditures in order to manage commitments. The shock of Suez had not resulted in any far-reaching or thorough re-evaluations of the national position. The new government under Prime Minister Macmillan made active efforts to establish better relations with the United States. The basic weakness of Britain's economy, however, meant that it would no longer be possible to occupy the position which had been maintained for a decade after the Second World War.

The decision to stress nuclear weapons also left Britain vulnerable.

In reality, great expense was involved, and there was lack of margin for failure, which meant that the British would be forced into further dependence upon American military decisions. The British made progress in hydrogen bomb development, and exploded their first device in 1957. In 1958, the McMahon Act was amended to permit supplying nuclear information to Britain. Nevertheless, the situation inherently contained the potential for embarrassment and misunderstanding, and in fact in the early 1960s led to the second great crisis in postwar Anglo-American relations. In 1960, the Blue Streak missile was cancelled. It had not only proved to be far more expensive than anticipated; it was also clearly obsolete even before final development was reached. Liquid-fuel missiles such as Blue Streak were inferior to those using solid fuel, which was much less volatile and facilitated rapid launching. The decision to cancel caused concern but not alarm in Britain, thanks to the expectation that the nuclear deterrent would be maintained through use of the American Skybolt missile. Skybolt would fill the time gap until Blue Steel was ready for use. President Eisenhower had agreed to provide the system in informal talks with Macmillan, and British confidence concerning American intentions carried over into the Kennedy Administration.

President Kennedy and his advisers, however, perceived the situation differently. No formal commitment had been made to deliver the system. Moreover, Secretary of Defense McNamara and others developed serious doubts about the advantages to be gained from the weapon. When compared with other weapon systems in terms of economy and efficiency, Skybolt was seen to be lacking. In a decision which strongly reflected these sorts of straightforward cost-effectiveness considerations, and without regard to British sensitivities or the central role they envisioned for the weapon, Skybolt was cancelled. By all accounts, the Americans were surprised by the intensity of British reaction to the move. On its own terms and within the given context, the decision was not only defensible but highly desirable. The problem was that other diplomatic and political considerations/had not been weighed in the calculation. The British, assuming confidently that there was no misperception of intentions by either side, believed that all was well up until the time of cancellation. The ensuing British reaction to cancellation led directly to talks between Kennedy and Prime Minister Macmillan at Nassau in December 1962. It was agreed that, as a compromise, the Americans would provide Polaris missiles and related technical information, and that the British would construct missile-firing submarines and nuclear warheads to go with them. The resolution of the crisis did enable the British to remain within the nuclear weapons club, but at a considerable price. Even the comparatively few submarines planned for the programme—a total of five—would be enormously expensive, and were not to be ready until the late 1960s, leaving a period of several years during which the V-bombers would be largely ineffective with no alternative deterrent operative. There was also the point, more basic and important, that the entire British deterrent programme could be shattered by a comparatively minor American weapon decision. Again, British decline from independent great-power status was underlined.[18]

It was also during the early 1960s that the NATO nations discussed among themselves the feasibility and practicality of the American initiative to develop a Multilateral Force (MLF) of nuclear-armed ships to be manned by crews from different Alliance nations. The scheme had originated among a group of planners in the State Department as a device for limiting the proliferation of nuclear weapons by providing participation in a nuclear force to other nations within the Atlantic area. The weapons would only be fired upon agreement among all the countries involved that they were to be used.

There were a number of problems, practical as well as political, which caused controversy about the scheme. First, there was the clumsiness inherent in manning a warship with men from different navies and countries, speaking different languages, possessing different cultural backgrounds and outlooks. For this reason, it was ultimately decided to create a force of surface ships rather than submarines. Second, the force would consist of only a very small part of the American nuclear deterrent, and thus of NATO nuclear strength. In effect, therefore, fundamental decisions concerning use of nuclear weapons would remain in American hands. The US had a veto on use of MLF missiles as a participant in the force; the special fleet of ships was too small and insignificant to make it central to decisions about nuclear war. This all gave an artificial quality to the fleet, and an image of the Americans being transparently deceptive in bringing forward a proposal which did not involve any really substantial sharing of power over the decision to use nuclear weapons.[19]

For the purpose of this analysis, an important feature of the MLF is the lack of significant intervention or influence by the British. Britain, along with France, was one of three members of the Alliance possessing a nuclear capability. This, combined with emphasis on close American ties, might have led the British to play a decisive role, presumably one which would have involved pointing out the weaknesses of the scheme at an early stage. Certainly in earlier decades they had employed their special and pivotal position to ease differences and facilitate communication between the rest of Western Europe and the US. In this case, however, the British were both cautious and peripheral to events. Prime Minister Wilson in 1964 proposed an Atlantic nuclear force, which contained some slight modifications and variations from the MLF proposal. Basically, however, the British did not have great impact on either the genesis or the resolution of the initiative.[20]

The Wilson government, elected in 1964, did have an important impact on British defence policy, however, thanks to the review carried out under Defence Minister Denis Healey. To a degree, the results of this examination were very generally similar to the earlier Sandys exercise. No major revolution in the profile of military forces was proposed; instead, there were to be a variety of different sorts of cuts, which would affect all the services. The British army was to be reduced from 180,000 to about 165,000 men, following the end of the Indonesian–Malaysia conflict in which British troops were engaged. Concerning sea power, the Healey report decided against a proposed third aircraft carrier. Further, it was concluded that the entire carrier force would be taken out of service by 1975. This, in turn, had significant implications for the air force, since it would effectively limit operations to land bases.[21]

The Healey White Paper departed from Sandys, however, in outlining reductions of commitments as well as forces. To be sure, debate in Parliament and other public statements about the reductions minimised their impact on Britain's international position and prestige. Healey himself became at times quite strident in describing the significant role which remained to the nation even after reductions. Critics of British defence policies have seized on such statements as proof of failure to accept and abide by reality. Waltz is especially caustic in tone:

> In the early 1960s the rhetoric of contribution and influence became more and more bewildering: to derive influence from a nuclear force while depending for component parts upon another country; to pose as a first-class power by maintaining a third-rate military establishment; to play a global role with the world's seventh-ranking army. The first Wilson government reacted not so much by making a decision as by uttering a confession. Britain will continue to seek a

measure of control over the resources of others, especially those of
the United States, and this will presumably continue to be adver-
tised as exercising influence or more generally as "giving a lead".
. . . Britain can initiate small military actions only to draw others
in if they are not quickly ended. . . .[22]

Nevertheless, beneath rhetorical reaffirmations of greatness, the
British were significantly cutting back on international commitments.
Evacuations of Singapore, Malaysia and Aden were planned. The
continuing emergency in Malaysia slowed down withdrawal there, and
conflict in Aden in 1969 brought in British military help. As these
events unfolded, it was shown both that the British were drawing in
what had become very extended lines of support, and that they were
capable of providing effective combat assistance to allies who called
for aid in small conflicts. With the Healey White Paper, the British
were stressing a new awareness of and sensitivity to the limits of the
nation. Statements emphasised that Britain would avoid becoming
engaged in overseas conflicts which could not be entered in conjunc-
tion with allies. Additionally, the British pledged explicitly not to
intervene in situations where they lacked substantial local support, or
to remain in bases in other countries which had requested them to
withdraw. The hallmark of British foreign policy has always been a
willingness to move, albeit gradually, with shifting events. The 1965–6
defence review indicated awareness that the international power con-
figuration dictated a much more limited and restrained role.[23]

There was no significant change in defence policy with the advent of
the Heath government in 1970. Some elements in the Conservative
Party had been especially anxious during the latter part of the 1960s to
increase defence spending. Once in office, however, the main quality
of policy was continuity with the past. Some care was taken to preserve
the names and independent identities of old regiments; but overall
force levels continued to go down gradually under the pressure of
economic conditions. As one knowledgeable analyst put it recently:
"Despite the promise of the Conservative government in 1970 to
reverse the previous government's reshaping of the British defence
effort, the budgets of 1971–3 did little to add to existing defence
capabilities", adding that the few changes made "were largely
cosmetic". The last budget of the Heath government cut defence
spending by seven per cent.[24]

The Labour government which took office early in 1974 made
substantial defence cuts. A broad review, comparable to those under

Sandys and Healey, was completed in 1975 and resulted in a decision to reduce spending by £200 million over five years. This cutback completed the process of British global withdrawal and increasing focus on Europe. The political decision to remain within the EEC, made final by the referendum of 1975, was complemented by the direction of defence policy.[25]

BRITISH AND AMERICAN STRATEGIES

Throughout the period since the Second World War, there have been important differences between Britain and the United States in approaches to international strategic and military issues. These have gone beyond simply reflecting the fact that one nation has been declining while the other has been rising to an ascendent position. The purpose of this section is to outline and clarify these contrasts, and to discuss them in terms of different institutional, cultural and historical backgrounds. In many ways, examination of strategic issues leads to conclusions very similar to those resulting from consideration of more general qualities of the two political systems.

The British approach to military policy has lacked the American preference for conceptual complexity, precision and clear objectives. Where the Americans have favoured quantitative and other schematic techniques, often quite abstract, for analysis and prescription concerning strategic policy, the British have preferred to operate with more traditional ideas about engaging military forces. The Americans have shifted dramatically, and sometimes quite abruptly, between emphasis on conventional or nuclear capabilities. The British have been much more inclined to view the two kinds of military forces as complementary rather than competitive; and, while their doctrines have changed over time, they have not been given to making the enormous strategic leaps characteristic of the Americans. Policy-makers in the US, confronted with a markedly changed position after the Second World War, have oscillated for years between fear of Soviet power and a desire to reshape the international environment drastically. In defence and strategic policy, as in diplomacy generally, the British have tried to employ their techniques of working within and adjusting to the *status quo* at the margins, even though the international system is markedly different from what it was before the Second World War.

To describe differences is not to deny similarities or mutual influence. In fact, there have been a number of parallels between the two nations on defence policy. As Samuel Huntington has described, the British at times have led the way in strategic shifts which were later adopted by the Americans. The Eisenhower "New Look" of 1954 was preceded by a similar change in doctrine on the part of Prime Minister Churchill and his military chiefs. The reduction of reserves in Britain in 1955 was followed by an American decision to follow the same course two years later. The tendency for the British to provide the lead in manpower policies, though less apparent, was still detectable. The abolition of conscription in Britain in 1960 anticipated the American move to a volunteer army a decade later.[26]

Nevertheless, this very general similarity in broad movements in military policy has been accompanied by a large number of contrasts in emphasis and approach. The American New Look stressed the tremendous destructive power of atomic weapons, with a complementary drastic reduction in conventional forces. British policy during the same period recognised atomic weapons as holding primary importance, but did not allow this to overshadow conventional weapons in the same manner. The Sandys report was a major policy statement which led to significant force reductions, but was not characterised by the sort of complex conceptual discussions of strategic theory typical of American debate on the subject. During the early 1960s in Britain, there was nothing like the sharp American reversal from a formal commitment to "massive retaliation" to an equally precise adoption of "flexible response". More important, the substantial American build-up in conventional strength in the early 1960s contrasts with the continuation of a steady reduction in British force levels. In 1961, the British were able to cope with the Berlin crisis only by extending the terms of conscripts left in the military. This leads back to the more general point that the United States has moved, at times very quickly, from one viewpoint to another on strategic policy. The British have changed more gradually and predictably, without either the sudden shifts of policy or emphasis on doctrinal clarity which have been characteristic of their principal ally.

These contrasting strategic styles are generally in line with the different policy-making traditions and structures in Britain and the United States which have already been discussed. In the US, academics and other professionals outside government have had much more ready and easy access to positions of power and influence in policy-making. This, in turn, has had at least two important implications for defence affairs. First, the same sort of comparative diversity of view and freshness of approach brought by staff turnover in

American government generally at the national level has applied to the specific field of foreign affairs. In both Britain and the US, the foreign service may be organisationally, psychologically and sociologically separate from the rest of the career professionals in the government; but in the US, in foreign as well as domestic affairs, there has also been an opportunity for outsiders to assume positions of influence at various levels within the bureaucracy. One of the most significant examples in American government of academic theory having an impact on public policy has occurred in military and strategic affairs, where theorists have had their jargon, concepts and arguments adopted, at least to a degree, by officials responsible for defence and foreign policy. Indeed, one of the frustrations over time in bilateral US–Soviet talks on limiting the arms race has been the discrepancy between the comparatively sophisticated American negotiators—in strategic theory terms—and their counterparts on the other side. Strategic and arms control studies, therefore, may be said to have influenced the practical policy field, even if they have not led to consensus on the important issues involved.

Second, from the opposite perspective, the comparative openness of American government may be cited as an important spur to the development of the field of strategic studies. Large numbers of scientists, and increasing numbers of social scientists, have since the Second World War been involved in advising government decision-makers, and serving in line positions as well, concerned with defence and military policy. In contrast to the situation in Britain, American academics have over the last few decades been closely and intimately involved with enormously complicated and revolutionary types of weapons. Doubtless a large number of factors must be cited in any complete analysis of the reasons for the development of an active and creative strategic studies community in the United States. Nevertheless, the direct engagement of such a significant number of these "outsiders" in the policy process itself cannot be underestimated.

On an organisational level, more specific features of defence policy-making in Britain and the United States reinforce the general points already made. In both countries, the 1960s witnessed efforts to use modern management tools to provide greater control over defence spending and the directions of military and strategic policy. Systematic quantitative analysis, generally known as Planning Programming Budgeting (PPB) was brought into the Pentagon by Secretary of Defense Robert McNamara in 1961. Soon thereafter, Britain went through a similar reform, with emphasis placed on using these new management tools to control defence expenditure. In broad terms, therefore, techniques for guiding defence policy were moving in the same direction in both countries. At the same time, nevertheless, there were different outcomes. In the US, emphasis on formal centralisation led to increasing conflict between McNamara and the services. In Britain, on the other hand, a much more centralised system of control was actually achieved. Understanding this contrast requires discussion of the more general organisational environment which surrounds defence policy.

Throughout the 1960s in the US, there was a constant and increasingly ambiguous conflict between the Secretary of Defense and the military service chiefs. At first, McNamara was able to impose strong central control over Pentagon policies and spending levels. His new, generally quite young staff successfully employed systems analysis to gain leverage over policy development and implementation within the Pentagon. These same reforms, however, also created an alliance among the services, which had previously been divided competitors, struggling for the largest slice of the defence budget pie. Under McNamara, tensions were strong between the military chiefs on the one hand, and the Secretary and his civilian staff on the other. In more concrete budgetary terms, the reforms of the new civilian leadership removed the vertical divisions between the military services, replacing them with a series of horizontal functional ones. The distinctions between the services were blurred by the focus, across service lines, on different types of equipment and supply, different purposes, and other analytical categories. The impact of the style of the new leadership combined with budgetary changes to unify the services and enlarge the gulf between them and their civilian heads.

Moreover, the American budgetary process has remained decentralised, and this has had an important bearing on defence policy. There are various power centres which have an impact on the policy process. In the US, the independence of Congress means that the executive branch officials lack the capacity to make truly decisive and unhampered decisions on budgetary matters. Rather, while institutions are separate, for this very reason there is continual interplay and mutual influence in the process of reaching final decisions on funds to be supplied to particular departments, and on the policies which will receive emphasis. In concrete terms, this means that military chiefs, technically under the direction of civilian leaders in the Pentagon and White House, have an important source of appeal and leverage concerning executive decisions within Congress. There are close ties between the military and powerful Congressional committees, especially the Armed Services and Appropriations committees. Again, the changes of the 1960s shifted previous relationships in this sphere. There was continuing tension between high Administration officials and the powerful Congressional committee chairmen who had an important voice in determining budgets and spending levels.[27]

There have been comparatively few direct and intense clashes between Congress and the executive over military policy. On the other hand, there has been a continuing, more restrained conflict, with constant legislative efforts to guide and define the directions of policy. As Huntington described the situation, writing before the McNamara years at the Pentagon:

> The unwillingness of Congress to exercise a veto over strategic programs does not mean that Congress has no role in the formulation of these programs. On the contrary, with strategy Congress has, like Bagehot's queen, "the right to be consulted, the right to encourage, the right to warn". The most prominent congressional role is that of prodder, or goad, of the Administration on behalf of specific programs or activities. With the executive the decision-maker, Congress becomes the lobbyist.[28]

During McNamara's tenure, relations with Congress became more difficult, and over time other barriers were raised against policy goals. The military services became increasingly adept at using systems analysis to promote their positions and views. A tool which had been employed to exercise greater control over the military was shown to be equally amenable to the opposite purpose. The primary innovation of the period in the Pentagon, therefore, was blunted and limited in its effectiveness. Moreover, the structural situation within the political system, where there were Congressmen who were both powerful and independent of the executive, meant that opponents of the Secretary's proposals had a ready arena in which policies could be contested and effectively opposed.[29]

The advent of a Republican Administration in 1969 brought a return to earlier defence budgeting procedures. In place of the continuing controversy under McNamara about the power of the Secretary of Defense and his immediate staff, and the strong division between the top of the hierarchy and the service chiefs, more traditional divisions between the different services re-emerged. The Joint Chiefs of Staff and the civilian secretaries of the military services were given more influence. Secretary of Defense Laird returned to the practice by which the head of the Department served as arbiter among the services in the struggle of each for a larger share of defence resources. The systems analysis staff was abolished, providing practical evidence that the politics of bargaining among divided services was once again the principal means for maintaining civilian control over the defence establishments.[30]

In Britain, structures for policy development and decision-making, and legislative–executive relationships generally, are much different, with the result of significant contrasts to the American experience. Generally, the greater centralisation, unity and co-ordination of British government has facilitated more effective control of the military, with less disruption and fewer departures from the *status quo* in policy. Once again, attention is drawn to the Treasury and its important role in decisions on annual expenditures. The position of the Treasury, combined with the unitary character of British government, involving effective fusion of Cabinet and Parliament, has facilitated the process of increased centralisation.

In general terms, developments in British defence organisation in the 1950s and 1960s paralleled changes taking place in the US. During the 1950s, a number of attempts were made through legislation to enhance the power of the American Defense Secretary, with perhaps the most significant being the Defense Reorganization Act of 1958. These were not very successful, and it was only during the McNamara years that really great shifts in power relationships occurred. In Britain, similar initiatives during the same decade to strengthen the Secretary of State for Defence were not of great consequence. As Richard Burt states in a recent, very thorough comparison of changes in British and American defence policies:

> Like the legislative reforms of the 1950s in the United States, these pronouncements did little to provide the Minister for Defence with the instruments with which to make budgetary decisions. During this period defence budget allocations on both sides of the Atlantic more often than not did not reflect any overall policy orientation, but [were] more the product of service bargaining and compromise.[31]

With the 1960s, the British began a much more determined drive to centralise defence policy. In 1963, an important White Paper on Central Organisation for Defence outlined reforms to create much greater cohesion and single direction to defence efforts. Following the changes outlined therein, the ministries of the Army, Navy and Air Force were reduced to the status of departments which were clearly subordinate to an inclusive Defence Ministry. Reflecting the sort of changes which were taking place under McNamara in the US, the powers of the military chiefs were curtailed, and ministers with new functional, rather than service, roles were moved to the fore. A special analytical body was established to undertake comparatively long-term budgetary planning. Throughout the 1960s, there was consistent emphasis on integration, and further blurring of lines dividing both ministers and civil servants responsible for the different military services. Again paralleling somewhat developments in the United States, the Conservative government elected in 1970 made an effort to revive distinctions between the service ministers. The reversal in course, however, to the extent that it occurred at all, was very weak.[32]

BROADER POLITICAL ENVIRONMENT

During the same period, changes were taking place in the Treasury which had an important bearing on defence policy. In 1961, the Treasury was significantly strengthened through the introduction of the Public Expenditure Survey (PES). This is a device for increasing control over government spending through very thorough review of budgetary plans, based on the principal of rolling five-year projections of expenditure. A high-level committee, chaired by a senior Treasury official, directs the PES. This reform has not removed the traditional atmosphere or practices of Treasury dealings with other government departments. There is still an emphasis on compromise, complex and at times almost ritualistic negotiations, involving the departments and ministers having policy disagreements. What the PES has done is to increase substantially the expertise, and therefore the negotiating leverage, of Treasury officials. Two American analysts of the British budgetary process, Hugh Heclo and Aaron Wildavsky, have gone so far as to declare that the Public Expenditure Survey is unrivalled by systems in other Western countries for control and analysis of public expenditure.[33]

Additionally, the British Parliament has contrasted markedly with the American Congress in terms of influence on defence policy and budgetary decisions. As noted earlier, Parliament has not provided an independent power base and challenge to executive authority comparable to the American Congress. To be sure, Parliament does have a Comptroller and Auditor General, whose functions are very similar to those of the very effective Comptroller General in the US. Consequently, there is an opportunity for legislative review of the costs and effectiveness of programmes after they are brought into being. On the other hand, Parliament notably lacks the very substantial staff resources available to Congressional committees at the stage when legislation is being considered. During Parliamentary sessions, a number of days—supply days—are allocated for discussion of government spending plans. However, and understandably, these normally are used for general debates on the wisdom of policy, rather than specific analysis of the details of policies. Despite the fact that comparatively large amounts of resources are devoted to defence, the dominant features of Parliamentary review—an emphasis on general issues and overviews of policy—are apparent in discussions of this policy sector as in others.[34]

It should also be emphasised that there were significant differences between Britain and the US in terms of the economic environment in which defence policy was made during the 1960s. McNamara's efforts at reform were suspect in military circles from the beginning, and aroused substantial political opposition. Nevertheless, resistance was diluted at least somewhat because of the fact that American defence expenditures were also rising during this period. Various factors encouraged this growth, including a generally expanding economy, the doctrinal shift from massive retaliation to flexible response, the general perception of the Soviet Union as a very threatening power, the related desire of officials in the new Administration to pursue a more aggressive and effective anti-Communist foreign policy, and specific international crises and reversals bearing on that foreign policy. In 1961, for example, American policy-makers were concerned about a variety of trouble spots, including Cuba, Berlin and Laos. The fact that the defence budget was expanding facilitated imposition of formal controls on the services and amalgamation along functional lines, since no particular military interest was financially threatened. Resources might be viewed as scarce when compared to an abstract ideal of what was really necessary for security, but in relative terms, when compared with the budgets of the Eisenhower years, they were quite plentiful. Left unresolved, therefore, was the question of how well the new system would survive in the American policy-making and institutional environment during a period of steady or diminishing budget levels. In the American context, one would justifiably expect strong and influential military opposition to unification plans, and such opposition to be especially great during a period of reduced resources.

In Britain, a very different economic situation prevailed during the 1960s and later. After 1964, the British were faced with the necessity of reducing defence spending in the light of growing economic problems. A range of commitments around the world, which in formal terms were quite extensive and—if all honoured—could prove an enormous drain, had to be cut back. Consequently, the story of British defence policy since the mid-1950s has been one of steady though gradual reductions in response to these pressures. Hard choices had to be made, for a number of years, between defence and other domestic policy priorities. Only very recently, in the wake of the costly and frustrating Vietnam War, has it become common in the US to question whether or not the nation has the capacity to achieve ambitious international goals. The British have had to face this question of serious national limitations since the end of the Second World War.

In institutional terms, this led to significant contrasts with the American situation. In the US, an expanding economy in the early 1960s permitted an expanding defence budget. This in turn mitigated, though hardly eliminated, military resistance to the McNamara reforms. In Britain, where there is no comparable Congressional independence to challenge the executive directly, and where the national bureaucracy is itself more unified and cohesive, it was much easier to impose central direction from above in defence and security affairs. In responding to economic imperatives, policy-makers had far more leverage in imposing their will on subordinates.

Finally on the list of contrasts, the popular political environment in which defence policy is made has been different in each country. Generally, defence policy conflicts within the domestic political system have carried much more force in the US than in Britain. This is not to suggest that defence policy has not been a source of controversy in Britain. Rather, policy-makers in the US have generally been more sensitive than those in Britain to this dimension of criticism. In Britain, there was through the 1950s continuing public debate about the appropriateness, and indeed the morality, of the nuclear deterrent. After Suez, the Campaign for Nuclear Disarmament became a major popular interest group, capable of mobilising very substantial demonstrations and marches. Throughout the decade, and into the early 1960s, the left wing of the Labour Party was largely opposed to continuation of the British nuclear force and favoured unilateral disarmament. At the 1960 Labour Party conference, the left was able to pass a resolution formally committing the party to this policy. Hugh

Gaitskell and other party moderates were able to dilute the impact of this victory, but only with considerable effort and compromise.[35]

Nevertheless, while this protest may have been very visible and strongly motivated, it did not result in anything resembling a major shift in national policy. Controversy was quite vociferous within the Labour Party, and at times entered Parliament as well. However, the nation continued to maintain a nuclear force. The return of Labour to government power in 1964 understandably raised some fears among those committed to established defence policies. These proved to be unnecessary; the Parliamentary Labour Party had specifically refused to be bound by the 1960 unilateralist resolution, and as already described, the defence policies of the Wilson years were broadly consistent with postwar trends.

In the US, on the other hand, defence policy, and a range of military and strategic concerns, have been prominent domestic political issues, especially during election campaigns. The cost of defence, despite the larger and stronger American economy, has been a continuing subject of debate. The Eisenhower Administration was attracted to the "New Look" policy largely because it promised to provide military security without enormous economic cost. In the late 1950s a group of Democratic Senators took up the cause of increased defence spending, motivated by fears of more ominous Soviet capabilities. John F. Kennedy made the issue a central one in his 1960 Presidential campaign. More generally, concern about Soviet intentions has ensured that strategic concerns would be of continuing prominence in American public discussion and political debate. From the outset of the Cold War, the image of a very threatening Soviet Union has been employed by those anxious to increase defence appropriations. During the early part of the Cold War, in the late 1940s and early 1950s, this same fear inspired Senator Joseph McCarthy's anti-Communist campaign. Again, defence and military considerations played an important role. McCarthy eventually turned his attention in public investigation from the State Department to the Pentagon, and specifically the Army's hierarchy. It was his attack on the military which ultimately discredited him publicly. In Britain, defence policy has largely escaped such bitter controversies about spending levels, and certainly regarding loyalty.[36]

STRATEGIC CHANGES AND NATIONAL RESPONSES

In summary, consideration of British and American military and strategic policies reinforces general points made earlier about differences in the foreign policies of the two nations. Both nations have existed in the same general international system since the Second World War, but have undergone different changes in position, and their national policies and attitudes have been defined by much different historical experiences. The Americans have had to become accustomed to loss of the protection provided by two oceans, and the isolation which enabled them to operate as a comfortable observer of international relations, intervening in the affairs of other nations selectively and by choice. The struggle to define American foreign policy has been reflected in the effort to outline clearly appropriate defence policies. The British have had to adjust to a position of inferiority which was not obvious—but was implicit and detectable—just after the Second World War, explicit and unavoidable in more recent years. In contracting their position and commitments in the system, the British have been able to get by through reliance on their established approach to international relations. The Americans have groped for a new concept of themselves in the global international environment; the British have relied on traditional empiricism, reacting to the most immediate crises, responding to pressures external to themselves, adjusting to circumstances while avoiding comprehensively detailed conceptions of their role. In this sense, both nations have been strongly influenced by their relationship to the wider Atlantic Area of nations. The US for most of the postwar period tried to translate very effective involvement in the NATO security arrangement into similar mutual defence arrangements with nations in other, more culturally distant regions of the globe. The British have gradually abandoned ambitions and pretensions for a sweeping international strategic role, finally focusing their efforts realistically on the European region of which they are undeniably a part.

Defence policies have mirrored international predispositions. The British have been slowmoving but consistent in reducing defence spending; the Americans have oscillated much more in the resources they have been willing to devote to the defence effort. Table 3.1 provides graphic evidence for this contrast. The British have tried to have as much as they could afford, spread among different capabilities. As a result, they have not had the conventional capacity to match that of the West Germans, or the same nuclear power emphasis as the French, while spending a much larger proportion of their gross national product on defence than either of these two. The Americans have not faced economic pressures comparable to those on the British, and no such constraints at all of any significance until very recent years;

TABLE 3.1: *Defence Expenditures: Britain and US*

Year	Britain	United States
1960	100.6	76.5
1961	100.6	79.6
1962	102.3	86.4
1963	103.5	85.1
1964	107.2	82.4
1965	107.0	82.1
1966	106.0	97.6
1967	109.3	112.7
1968	106.9	115.7
1969	100.2	110.8
1970	100.0	100.0
1971	105.2	92.3
1972	113.7	92.6
1973	112.0	88.1
1974	114.3	85.3

(Source: *The Military Balance 1975–1976*, International Institute for Strategic Studies, p. 80. Figures reflect local currency values with 1970 = 100. These are constant prices based on consumer price indices)

the restraints of the Eisenhower years were, in this sense, self-imposed. On the other hand, American strategic policy has been more uneven, more inconsistent over time. Economic conditions only provide the environment in which other factors are brought to bear.

Institutional structures and practices have both defined the respective approaches to security concerns. In the United States, there is comparatively more turnover of public officials, with a greater likelihood that a change of government will bring a marked shift in policy. In the US also, cultural predispositions toward clarity and precision in policy, faith in technology, and a desire for decisiveness in outcomes have all encouraged an approach towards strategic matters which has been both less predictable over time, and less ambiguous at any particular time, than that of the British.

It is not at all certain that the superpower's style is the best. In the wake of the Vietnam disaster, the United States is in unfamiliar new territory conceptually, struggling to define clearly a new international position, one more sophisticated than the earlier effort to contain and oppose a Communist threat which was seen as generally the same even if not structurally monolithic. The continuing Soviet–American interchange over *détente* is a combination of accord and hostility which is uncomfortable for a nation used to sharp distinctions between friendship and opposition. Britain has slowly but steadily reduced commitments to correspond with capabilities, and accepted the reality that the future lies in Europe, and to some extent the large Atlantic Area, rather than the world at large. It is arguable that Britain has accepted new realities more gracefully, with less frustration and domestic division, than the United States.

4 Britain and Europe

In 1961, Prime Minister Macmillan announced that the longstanding British policy of aloofness from the European Economic Community had been reversed, and application was made for membership. The change in course was significant not only for the fact that a European power of the stature of France or West Germany was seeking to join, but also because the reversal in policy was so sharp and complete. After all, when the Community was first established with the Treaty of Rome in 1957, the British had reacted not only with aloofness but also active opposition. The nation had the opportunity to join and did not. Moreover, there was an effort to oppose the new formation through support for competing conceptions of a general free trade area, and, later, of the European Free Trade Association. In this sense, the British were turning to join a specific organisation which had been strongly opposed in the past.

More generally, the effort to enter Europe was a reversal not only of immediate past policy, but also, as we have seen, of a much longer-term and historically based aversion to intimate continuing involvement in European affairs. The notion of being explicitly and formally linked to economic institutions, which were themselves based on ambitions for supranational political integration, was alien to the British approach of influencing European events without becoming decisively enmeshed in them.

In both short- and long-term perspectives, therefore, the move to enter Europe highlighted the position of Britain and the manner in which that position has changed since the Second World War. The decision to seek membership, and the continued efforts to do so after initial rebuff by de Gaulle in 1963, aptly reflect British movement from the status of being an important, global, international power to a more modest regional one. As Britain's traditional ambitions became an increasing burden, a burden which could not be maintained, there was a retreat to a concentrated focus on Europe as the region of principal concern.

The unexpected abruptness of the British public announcement to seek entry into the Community in 1961 might be taken to imply that the decision was made at the top, without broad consultation throughout the government or the interested larger public community. To some extent, this is true, but only in the most narrow sense that a good deal of initiative on the matter, including the final judgement itself, rested with the Prime Minister. At the same time, the application for Community membership, and the persistence—over a long period of time—to carry through that policy despite two rebuffs and the alteration of the parties in government, reflects a more complex process of interchange, debate, and shift of attitudes within various sectors of the British government and wider political systems.

This chapter discusses the issue of Common Market entry from this perspective, with special attention to the role of domestic politics in this particular foreign policy, and also to the manner in which interest groups, political parties, and the civil service influenced policy. From the opposite perspective, there is also consideration of the apparent effects of Community membership on the functioning of public policy machinery. In contrast to defence and security issues, and to those relating to co-ordination and organisation of government departments for the conduct of foreign policy, there are no simple or clear opportunities for detailed comparisons and contrasts with American structures, policies and practices on this issue. At the same time, this subject does relate directly to the general position and role of Britain within the Atlantic Area. In one sense, entry into Europe is evidence of British recognition of the inability to maintain a broad international involvement. From another related perspective, entry represents rejection of a narrow isolationist or parochial viewpoint on the world and acceptance of the sort of internationalism implied by commitment to Europe.

BRITAIN AND EUROPE AFTER THE SECOND WORLD WAR

As outlined and discussed earlier, Britain ended the war in a position which reinforced traditional foreign policy attitudes rather than encouraging new departures. Britain had been one of the victors; most of the major nations of Europe had been defeated during the course of the conflict. The Empire and Commonwealth were largely intact, and had rallied to the support of the mother country. Unlike France and Germany, the British were not compelled to rethink a new international role, did not have to face similar insecurities and uncertainties. Instead, the British were able to view themselves as being on a plane roughly equal to the United States and the Soviet Union, the two emerging superpowers of the postwar period. In practical and concrete policy terms, the British played an important role in firmly wedding the United States and Western Europe through the NATO Alliance, and in facilitating the implementation of the Marshall Plan. Flexibility, interest mixed with independence, influence without commitment; these historical attitudes toward Europe seemed to be serviceable and useful in the years just after the war as well.

Nevertheless, the immediate postwar period also brought economic problems for Britain. These difficulties had been developing for a long period of time, but in previous decades had been much easier to ignore. Now, they compelled a British retreat, witnessed first in the Mediterranean area, from a range of international commitments and involvements. The American attitude of driving a hard bargain for any economic aid to Britain, while at the same time showing open willingness to take up the ally's international burdens, encouraged this retreat.

Britain's attitude toward Europe generally reflected historical patterns of behaviour rather than these pressing economic problems. Gradual, steady international retreat began soon after the Second World War; a European focus was nevertheless steadfastly resisted. Economic problems were forcing a lesser world role; British finesse enabled the old diplomatic approaches to European affairs to be used successfully.

The desire of Britain to play a strong role in Europe without strong commitment to developing supranational institutions ultimately collided with the position of another sizeable power in the region— France, or more specifically, de Gaulle. This should not be taken to suggest that relations between these two extremely complex nations, with their long mutual history of alliance and opposition, were automatically difficult in any simple clearcut sense. In 1940, during the darkest period of the war for the Allies, Churchill, newly installed as Prime Minister in the wake of the discredited Chamberlain, suggested emotionally and melodramatically that Britain join with France to form a single nation, albeit under pressure resulting from German military victories on the Continent. With considerable irony, the impending collapse of France brought Churchill—one of the great nationalists of the time—to renounce this spirit, in which he was joined by de Gaulle, who was then trying desperately to continue a French presence in the war. De Gaulle, for his part, had at times expressed very great admiration for the British. The sweep and grandeur of British history, domestic as well as international, was appealing to the General, as was the conservatism and traditionalism of the political style and institutions. Often he linked the "Anglo-Saxons" in expressing suspicion and condemnation; on the other hand, he also differentiated between the British and the Americans, having a distrust for the latter which he did not impose on the former.

Nevertheless, the dominant motif of British policy toward Europe during the years after the war was one which minimised the importance to foreign policy of involvement in that region. Churchill, in a famous Zurich speech of 1946, urged the creation of what he termed "a kind of United States of Europe". He also made it clear, however, that this new order was to follow the British conception of Europe, in other words only the nations of the Continent would be formal members. There was an emphasis on Europe as only one, and surely not the most important, of the three spheres of British influence and interest, along with the Commonwealth and the United States. [1]

As noted earlier, after the war Britain encouraged collaboration among Western nations while carefully keeping a distance. The OEEC, Brussels Pact, and NATO have all been cited as examples of Britain serving successfully as a catalyst. Organisations with more explicit and important supranational political overtones, however, such as the Council of Europe, the European Coal and Steel Community (ECSC), and of course the European Economic Community, were either joined only reluctantly or boycotted altogether. At times, very specific political considerations played a role in British decisions to remain apart. For example, when the European Coal and Steel Community initiative was taken, the Labour government at the time had just nationalised the coal industry and anticipated taking over steel as well. Consequently, there was a reluctance to surrender total national control over these industries to a new European authority. [2]

There was some anticipation in Continental circles that the new Conservative government elected in 1951 would be more sympathetic to the European cause. Churchill, after all, had often spoken enthusiastically, if vaguely, about European unification, and the party had formally come out in support of at least discussion of entry into the European Coal and Steel Community. Nevertheless, in power the Tories followed the Labour Party's attitude of caution and scepticism concerning European integration. The government was very tentative about the ECSC, limiting policy statements to general declarations of support and friendship for the new undertaking, while declining to ask for full membership. Of more moment and impact, the Conservatives also refused to join the new European Defence Community (EDC). This plan for a European army, designed in part to integrate and restrict the West Germans in the context of a broader military establishment, had been opposed by the Labour government. The Conservatives, however, while out of power had generally endorsed the plan and specifically advocated a form of British participation. It was therefore quite startling for the Europeans when the new British government reneged on what had been an informal but strong pledge and refused to join the EDC. Churchill made it clear in parliamentary debate that the British army would never be integrated with this ' organisation; general collaboration was declared to be sufficient. The EDC, weakened by lack of British support, was brought to an end by the refusal of an endorsement by the French Assembly in 1954.[3]

During the early 1950s, Foreign Secretary Eden tried other, more general and therefore congenial approaches to European co-operation. In 1952, he took the initiative to try to bring Britain and the Continent closer together by proposing early in the year that the Council of Europe be used as the basic umbrella organisation for more bodies with more specific functions and tasks. The Council would serve as the main forum and mechanism for communication and co-operation among the European governments. The British cause was obviously not helped by the refusal to participate in the EDC and the ECSC, and Eden's effort resulted in total failure. It was viewed on the Continent as a characteristic British attempt to gain the advantages of collaboration without suffering the costs and inconveniences of membership. Later, however, Eden enjoyed a substantial success in Europe. Following the final collapse of the EDC in 1954 he played a leading role in using the Western European Union as a device for promoting defence co-operation. Once again, the British were able to employ diplomacy in a catalytic way to foster useful collaboration among European states. Also in line with the historical British approach, links were forged which did not involve any surrender of fundamental national sovereignty.[4]

This was the background to the formation of the European Economic Community, which was the most far-reaching initiative of the several for Western European collaboration. In mid-1955, foreign ministers of the six nations which composed the ECSC met in Messina to discuss a much more comprehensive European community effort. These talks created the momentum which led to the Treaty of Rome, signed by the Six in 1957. The new Community institutions were established in 1958, with an agenda for building increasing collaboration and structural linkage among the participating nations. In short, it was considerably more ambitious than earlier arrangements. Rather than emphasising detailed rules for co-operation, the new entity was designed to lay the groundwork for broad political and economic integration. There were concrete plans concerning the establishment of a uniform customs net binding the members, but this was to be only the first step toward much more comprehensive political and economic unity among the European states.[5]

From the first the British had an opportunity to participate in this new enterprise, but chose to abstain. As early as 1949, there had been informal and quiet talks between representatives of the European movement, including Jean Monnet, and British government officials. These failed, mainly because the British concentrated on precise and narrow trade concerns, without accepting the broader European vision of unity. Monnet, rebuffed, turned away. As Robert Lieber, who has studied the British domestic politics of entry into the Community in an intensive manner, put it: "Once it was clear that British leaders such as Bevin, Morrison, and Attlee opposed association on anything more than a most-favored nation basis, Monnet determined to go ahead in his project without Britain."[6] The British sent only one observer to the Messina conference, and he was a low-ranking official on the Board of Trade. The new arrangements were too inclusive for British tastes, threatening the basic conception of independent nations operating in a flexible, shifting European environment.

During the second half of the 1950s, the British moved to increasing separation from and hostility to the new economic organisation. At first, there was an effort to dilute it through the proposed Free Trade Area. Later, there was clear opposition, expressed through formation of the competing European Free Trade Association (EFTA). British policy, though employing two different tools, was consistently loyal to the tradition of resisting solidification of power relationships on the Continent, especially through the formation of *blocs*.

The proposed Free Trade Area involved an associational relationship which had already been explored by representatives of other European states. The idea of a free trade arrangement among the nations of Europe had in fact been considered by the founders of the

EEC. In April 1956, Belgian Foreign Minister Paul-Henri Spaak presented a report to his colleagues from the other Community nations. A principal thrust in the document, understandably, was the importance of the new Community relationship among the Six. At the same time, however, there was attention to possibilities for non-members to become linked to the organisation. This in turn spurred interest in establishing such a broader set of relationships. In early 1957, an OEEC report was made public which recommended such a free trade area.[7]

In February 1957, the Conservative government issued a White Paper which put the basic British policy on the matter before the OEEC. Fundamentally, the British attempted in this document and the negotiations which followed to secure the benefits of participation in the Community without assuming any of the burdens and costs. They wished to create free trade for industrial goods among European countries. Tariffs and quotas therefore would be reduced. Beyond this, the British were unwilling to go. There was determination to protect special trade relationships with the Commonwealth, and to resist not only the supranational political ambitions of the new Community, but many of the economic ones as well. There was no intention of going beyond lowering industrial trade barriers to pursue more positive goals, such as detailed economic integration, harmonisation of social policy, or even the inclusion of agricultural goods. Clearly, the British were interested in retaining links to Europe, but equally were resistant to surrendering others which bound the nation to more distant parts of the world. As Waltz puts the matter: "The trick to be accomplished was to preserve England's role in the two circles of longer radii without being excluded from the developing European market."[8]

The very fact, however, that the British were trying to gain important advantages at virtually no cost created problems in the negotiations which followed, and ultimately this defeated the initiative. Agricultural members of the EEC strongly resented British insistence on opening the door to industrial trade with Europe while keeping the door for farm products closed. Over time, as Continental attitudes became clearer through the process of negotiations, the British became more flexible and accommodating. There was a recognition of the importance of agricultural arrangements, and concessions as well concerning broader economic integration and the supranational political goals of the Community. Nevertheless, this shift did not come quickly enough to save the British position. The

French were especially strong opponents of British association. The "free trade" conception was something they found grating. They were highly suspicious of British motives, and particularly of the insistence on maintaining the special trading relationship with the Commonwealth. In late 1958, President de Gaulle vetoed the British application. His agent, Jacques Soustelle, announced with finality that "it is not possible to create the Free Trade Area as wished by the British, that is with free trade between the Common Market and the rest of the OEEC but without a single external tariff barrier round the seventeen countries, and without harmonisation in the economic and social sphere".[9]

Following frustration of the free trade negotiations, the British turned actively to promotion of a competing *bloc* of nations, the European Free Trade Association or "Outer Seven". True to the balancing approach to international politics, British leaders endeavoured to neutralise the solidification and harmonisation of the policies of EEC countries by establishing a competing centre of power. The Community threatened to congeal the relationships among important European states, a notion antithetical to the British. The Community required clear British commitment to the new supranational institutions and goals, which again was out of tune with the nation's normal approach to European relations. The EFTA was designed to counterbalance these disturbing trends. It consisted of Britain, plus a diverse group of states—Austria, Portugal, Denmark, Norway, Sweden and Switzerland.

The formation of the EFTA really began almost immediately after the French veto of the Free Trade Area. At the beginning of December 1958, the Outer Seven met for preliminary talks in Geneva. Further, more intensive discussions were held in Oslo and Stockholm during the first part of 1959. There were other meetings in June, and in the interim Norwegian and Swedish representatives talked individually with the other governments involved. During that month, following a lengthy round of talks in Stockholm, it was agreed formally to begin the European Free Trade Association on 1 July 1960. This deadline was met with a twenty per cent tariff reduction among EFTA members.[10]

From the very start, the purpose of the new association was not to establish a continuing trading association, but rather to lever concessions out of the EEC. By making their overall economic position stronger, the excluded nations could minimise the effect of the new Community. The Outer Seven lacked the sort of trading, cultural and geographical ties which bound the EEC states together. The British goal was to weaken the EEC and further freer trade throughout Western Europe, not set up another permanent supranational organisation. The dangers and divisions facing the region with competition between the EEC and EFTA were emphasised by British diplomats in an effort to encourage conciliation and compromise.

In fact, the EFTA offensive served principally to harden EEC resolve and indicate the comparatively shaky position of the British. France, in particular, determined not to weaken in the face of British rigidity, did very little business with EFTA countries. The lowering of tariff barriers within the EEC provided a concrete benefit and firm incentive to hold the line. Generally, the EFTA lacked the economic strength and policy cohesion to provide a real challenge to the EEC. Finally, the effective transformation of the OEEC into the Organisation for Economic Co-operation and Development (OECD) in early 1960 brought North America more directly into the affairs of Europe. This further restricted the independent importance of the EFTA. Relatedly, the new organisation represented the important direct impact of the United States in Europe. In the context of this powerful reach, Britain was no longer in a position to play transatlantic catalyst.[11]

POLICY CHANGE

Faced with a failure of British attempts to weaken or dilute the EEC, Prime Minister Macmillan announced at the end of July 1961 that an effort would be made formally to join the organisation, and would involve greater sacrifice of independence than Britain hitherto had been willing to make. The economic ties with the Commonwealth, it was admitted, might have to be compromised in order to join the more intimate relationship with Europe. Once this change in policy occurred, Britain was committed to entry. National spokesmen might shift their tone and attitude on specific points, and question the wisdom of commitment to Europe, but there was no real retreat to the pre-1961 position of opposition. In this sense, the decision once made was maintained over time.

The negotiations with the Community, following the Macmillan declaration, were long, and ultimately the first round ended in disappointment for Britain. There was a deceptively positive quality to the atmosphere which greeted the British application. The EEC

Commission expressed "satisfaction" at the event. De Gaulle was quoted to the effect that the move was "good for Europe and good for the world".[12] Nevertheless, from the start it was clear to those who chose to look that a very large and serious gulf separated Britain from the Six. The British were determined to maintain Commonwealth preferences for which the Six had no more than short-term tolerance. To be sure, the British were prepared to compromise their position in order to gain admission; what ultimately did them in was the enormous morass of detail attending the talks, plus the final French decision that they should not be let in.

The talks stretched over a period of a year and a half. The British requested that they begin with a formal letter in August 1961. The resulting discussions continued until the French veto of January 1963. In anticipation of an expansion of the Community, Denmark and Norway applied for membership during the same period. It was on this optimistic note that the negotiations began, only to become bogged down almost immediately in the details of complex existing and proposed economic arrangements.

The Commonwealth represented an enormous barrier to agreement, which could be surmounted only slowly and by considerable effort. The British were caught between the existing bonds of this association, and determination to enter the Community. Commonwealth partners were applying pressure to keep trading preferences, while EEC nations were demanding that Britain would have to end them as a price of membership. The situation was addressed by taking up each commodity and other trading agenda item on an individual basis. In turn, this led to very lengthy, detailed and gruelling negotiations, the outcome of which often turned on small and seemingly trivial points. The French, who were important food producers, had a special interest in trying to get as much of the European market for themselves as possible and restricting Commonwealth competition. The result of the general situation was that there was no comprehensive agreement reached for EEC membership which the British were willing to accept.

British domestic agriculture presented an even more troublesome policy area, on which the negotiations eventually foundered. The British system of generous agricultural subsidies, which automatically maintained an artificial guaranteed price even when market prices were down, threatened Community farm producers, and again especially the French. The Europeans were afraid that British farmers would undersell them. While the British were willing eventually to conform to normal EEC agricultural arrangements on subsidies, they insisted upon a much longer period of transition than the Europeans were willing to grant. [13]

These were the events which made up the prelude to de Gaulle's historic press conference of mid-January 1963. At that time, the General declared that the British were insufficiently European, too closely tied to the United States. The informal but strong bonds within the Anglo-Saxon community, he believed, made it impossible for the British to be reliable members of the European organisations. The press conference was long, with some expression of bitterness toward the British. During this period, and not for the first or last time, there was clear division between France and the other five members of the Community, all of whom were sympathetic to British entry. At the final meeting of the foreign ministers of the Six, de Gaulle's minister, Couve de Murville, formally took the step of excluding the British, with the emphasis while so doing on the need to maintain the "European" integrity of the entity. If Britain came in, it was maintained, a large number of other states would soon follow. The real concern, of course, unspoken but recognised by all who attended this meeting, was that the British were too close to the United States, that a Community in which Britain was a member would be dominated by the Americans through this agency. The importance of the Anglo-American relationship to the course of British–Community relations will be developed more fully in the next chapter. Here, it is sufficient to note this was the unspoken but apparent factor in the French veto. [14]

The only development which might have saved the British position at this time would have been a move of strong support on the part of the West Germans, under Konrad Adenauer. But here, as elsewhere, de Gaulle was able to control the situation. Through adroit political manoeuvre, the General was able to ensure that relations were maintained with West Germany. Adenauer clearly put the highest priority on friendship and continued reconciliation with France. Between the January press conference and the decisive meeting of foreign ministers in Brussels, Adenauer journeyed to Paris to make the extremely important symbolic gesture of signing a friendship treaty with France. [15]

Not surprisingly, there was a sharp decline of British interest in the European Community after the veto, though this proved to be only temporary. The General's act had been something of a humiliation as well as a disappointment, made worse by the fact that it had been unexpected. The British did not clearly and explicitly declare themselves against the Community but did pay much less attention to it. The Common Market played virtually no role as a subject for debate and discussion during the 1964 general election. The Home government, which had succeeded Macmillan's in 1963, did not move to reopen negotiations; and it appeared that the Labour government of Harold Wilson, elected with the narrowest of margins in 1964, would continue to stay apart from Europe.

THE SECOND APPLICATION

By early 1965, however, the British once again had developed noticeable interest in joining Europe. There are several identifiable factors which bear on this change of attitude. The Community had been in a kind of doldrums following the General's veto. Since the other five members had supported British entry, what was a humiliation for the applicant was at least a disappointment for them. Late in 1964, however, agreement of a comprehensive nature was achieved on grain prices, which in turn breathed some new life into Community affairs. Also, there were certain negative factors encouraging a more explicit British turn toward Europe. A very serious balance-of-payments deficit developed in 1964, which resulted in the need to borrow a total of three billion dollars in November of that year. There were also significant problems in the aircraft industry. Finally, the Administration in Washington at this time was distinctly less appealing and congenial than its predecessor. Miriam Camps notes this point in her analysis of the development of the Community through the first half of the 1960s. The Kennedy Administration had a style and tone which appealed to Europeans, and many officials in Washington at that time placed the highest priority on relations across the Atlantic. The Johnson Administration was, on the other hand, increasingly preoccupied with events in Southeast Asia, and also represented an important attitudinal change: "President Johnson's style and approach are much more characteristically American . . . Unlike President Kennedy, he makes the British aware of the differences between his reactions and their reactions."[16]

More generally, it was increasingly clear as time passed that British trading patterns were developing naturally toward Europe and away from the Commonwealth. During the 1964 election campaign, the Labour Party had devoted some attention to expanding trade with the Commonwealth, but no such programme was defined or implemented after taking office. Moreover, a number of nations in the Commonwealth, including the important trading partners Australia and New Zealand, were seeking greater access not to the mother country, but to other nations in their own region of the world. Although trade with the Commonwealth had continued to grow into the first part of 1964, the trend drew to a close by the following year. Tariff discrimination against non-EEC members was beginning to have a strong effect. Finally, the expectations of really substantial reductions of trade restrictions among industrial nations as a result of the Kennedy Round negotiations were disappointed. The discussions were pursued through the middle of the decade, with the likelihood that some positive results would be achieved; but the great enthusiasm for free trade in the early 1960s, propelled by the Kennedy Administration, clearly had waned. [17]

The three political parties in Britain responded to these various considerations with revived interest in the Common Market. The Tories and Liberals were in the vanguard with advocacy of another effort to join a Community which was by then much more clearly an established, active, formidable organisation. The Liberals, the first to embrace Europe, had never really abandoned this sentiment, and it is therefore not surprising that they remained in the forefront on this issue. The Conservatives had lost their enthusiasm for Europe after the 1963 veto, but at this time rekindled it again. More explicitly than the Liberals, the Tories linked the European economic organisation to broader Atlantic political and security concerns, suggesting among other things that there could be a nuclear role for it after British entry. Conservative spokesmen, much more vigorously and precisely than in the past, stressed these political implications of Community membership. [18]

During 1965, the Labour Party also began to put greater emphasis on entering Europe, but still from a much more ambiguous posture. Labour formally favoured membership, but hedged this position with more conditions and greater reluctance than the other two parties. There was an emphasis on ensuring the protection of the domestic economy, reiterating the cautious policies the party had adopted during the abortive British accession negotiations a few years before. Also, there was a tendency to discuss entry in terms of serving as a bridge between the Six and the Outer Seven. [19]

In important ways, the Labour government was in a different position from the Conservatives when they had held power. Unlike the situation in the early 1960s, the governing party could count on support from the opposition in parliament. The obverse point, however, is that Labour, even in power, was divided on the issue as the Conservatives had not been. Wilson himself had been very ambiguous on the Common Market, and only slowly adjusted to a position of advocacy after becoming Prime Minister. A few key Cabinet changes soon after Labour took power were crucial in moving the new government in a pro-Market direction, reflecting the fragility of the policy.

The general election of 1966 was significant in this context. The Common Market was discussed in this election to an extensive degree, in contrast to the neglect of 1964. The Tory Party was by that time led by Edward Heath, the man who had served as principal negotiator during the abortive effort to enter the Common Market under Macmillan. Labour expressed general sympathy for the Community in the party election manifesto. More concretely, the party increased its majority in the election to a comfortable ninety-six seats, sufficient to permit pursuit of new and potentially controversial policy departures. As in 1964, a number of the new Labour MPs elected were pro-EEC.[20]

Armed with a solid majority, the government began to take increasing interest in a European initiative. While in opposition, the Labour Party had expressed interest in exploring various alternatives to the Community, with particular attention to the obvious candidates—the EFTA and the Commonwealth. Neither of these, however, proved suitable as a primary focus of government attention. At an EFTA meeting in the spring of 1965, Prime Minister Wilson tried to give increased impetus to the organisation. In a rather thoughtless fashion, the Labour government had imposed a fifteen per cent surcharge on EFTA imports the year before, in response to a very serious balance-of-payments crisis. One reason for this meeting, therefore, was to repair the diplomatic damage which had been done. This was largely accomplished. At the same time, the gathering also revealed that there was no strong sense of common interest or purpose to bind the members of the organisation. Originally, the British had established EFTA as a temporary body, designed as a tool to gain leverage on the European Community members. In the intervening years, it had assumed a limited independent existence, with success in reduction of trade barriers among the members. It never lost, however, the aura of a group which was principally instrumental to a larger end—that is, a more extensive European Economic Community. For this reason, it was extremely difficult to generate any sense of strong, explicit, distinctive enthusiasm for the organisation on the part of the members.[21]

The Commonwealth also proved insufficient to the task of providing Britain a base for a broader role in the international system. The British, as already discussed, have long ascribed a range of positive, and also vague and general, qualities to the Commonwealth. Waltz is only one of several analysts of British foreign policy who have been impressed by this feature of the approach to the Empire. To a degree, the viewpoint is quite understandable. Given the importance of the Empire to British economic and political power, it is not surprising that the Commonwealth should occupy a strong emotional and symbolic position in more recent perspectives on the international system.

In practical terms, however, there has been little to bind together the Commonwealth as an integrated set of nations, appropriate to serve as a primary focus for British foreign policy. Trade links had been declining as the British economy was drawn into Europe. Moreover, by the mid-1960s problems associated with British immigration policy created severe strains among Commonwealth nations. Racial problems grew in Britain, leading to more restrictive immigration policies. In turn, this created resentment among Commonwealth people who held British passports which were no longer valid. Therefore, the 1965 meeting of the Commonwealth nations, which was intended by Wilson to be a special opportunity to underline the importance of the body, turned out instead to be an unpleasant and somewhat acrimonious affair. Once again, with special force, the point was made that there was no special unity binding these nations. Frustrated elsewhere, Labour responded by turning toward Europe, attending to the diplomacy of getting along with Community nations, moving steadily toward a formal request for membership.

At about the same time, during the second half of 1965, the EEC was plunged into a serious crisis. An effort by the Commission, the executive headquarters of the EEC, to achieve supranational financial independence sparked a French walkout which threatened for a time to destroy the organisation. For the rest of the year, the EEC literally ceased to function, hanging in limbo as the membership worked to resolve the problem. Ultimately, early in 1966, the French were successful, and a compromise was reached. It included the important point that no independent financial powers were to be given the Commission.

Throughout the affair, the British maintained an attitude of careful, interested observer. The crisis was treated as very serious, as indeed it was, and worthy of attention. At the same time, care was taken not to intervene directly in the problems of a group to which Britain did not yet belong, lest the chances of entry be jeopardised.[22]

After the resolution of the Community crisis, the British began to move toward formal application for membership. In November, Prime Minister Wilson announced to parliament that a government review had concluded a new effort should be made to enter the organisation, and that preliminary discussions would be initiated at the top levels of each of the governments in the Six. A parliamentary resolution was passed in support of the effort. Soon thereafter, in the late spring of 1967, the government formally applied to join the Community, with membership to involve the ECSC and Euratom as well as the EEC. It is noteworthy that political along with economic considerations were stressed in the government's announcement of the move. Britain paid due respect to the broad goal of European political co-operation and integration as well as to the more concrete economic aspects.[23]

Almost immediately, scepticism about the appropriateness of British membership was voiced by de Gaulle, and ultimately the French once again vetoed the British application. At a press conference in mid-May, the General warned that Britain was insufficiently European to be considered for membership. Wilson pressed ahead, and following initial contacts received the approval of the Commission to begin negotiations. These never really got off the ground, however, for in late November de Gaulle announced finally that the British would not be allowed in.

Understandably, this resulted in another British reaction of aversion to and independence from the Community. For the third time in just under a decade, the British had been excluded—in a way, painfully snubbed—by the French. It seemed apparent that as long as General de Gaulle remained in power in France, no key could be devised which would unlock the door to the Community. British interest in membership waned, though economic and political realities urging association with the Six could not be completely ignored and would hardly be removed.

BRITISH ENTRY

Changes of government in both Britain and France created a more encouraging situation for Common Market membership as the 1970s began. After the domestic unrest of May 1968, and the resulting public referendum, de Gaulle left office. Pompidou, his successor, had also been his loyal deputy, but was nevertheless not viewed as a strong opponent of British entry into the EEC. In mid-1970, the Conservative Party was returned to power in Great Britain. Not only had there been a change of parties, but the new Prime Minister, Edward Heath, was noted both for particularly strong determination and a firm belief that Britain should be a member of the Community. Once again, the British began to probe possibilities for joining.

At approximately the same time, the Community members began to explore new possibilities for further development. There was a European summit conference at The Hague at the end of 1969. The agenda was comprehensive, and resulted in ambitious declarations concerning plans and anticipated progress for the future. Among the goals underlined was enlargement of the Community membership. The French did not oppose this. Indeed, various factors appear to have encouraged a marked change in attitude on their part. It was not only that de Gaulle was gone, or even that the new leadership was sensitive and uneasy about the isolation which he had brought to the nation's foreign policy. Beyond this, there was growing concern about the strength of West Germany. This nation was not only increasingly consequential in economic terms, but was also, under the new Social Democratic government of Willy Brandt, taking initiatives to reach accommodation with the Soviet Union and more generally with the Eastern *bloc.* For many years, the Americans and other West Europeans had been concerned that German desire for national reunification would lead to a settlement jeopardising the West's security. This old worry remained, and was combined with new ones about the growing pan-European influence of West Germany alone. The Erhard regime, following the friendly Adenauer years, had experienced some frictions with France, but there had nonetheless been nothing comparable to this new German diplomatic assertiveness and political strength. Enlarging the Community, therefore, was appealing as a way to strengthen it, help balance the Germans with the British, and perhaps tie the former more strongly to West Europe. Moreover, Brandt himself was committed to a stronger European Community.[24]

Three other nations applied simultaneously with Britain for Community membership—Denmark, Ireland and Norway. Ultimately, all joined except the last, where the Community was rejected in a popular referendum. Rather ironically in light of the results of the two previous British attempts to join the EEC, and particularly the very lengthy negotiations of 1961–3, difficulties attending entrance this time were handled very quickly and expeditiously. Within a year, all differences separating Britain and the Six were resolved. The pace of accomplishment was much faster for Britain than for the other three applicants.

In 1972, there was another European Summit, which again considered very comprehensive issues. The meeting was notable principally for the great progress made, going well beyond what had been anticipated. The earlier summit had resulted in a declaration that the "transition" phase of the Community had ended. The second meeting, reflecting a sense of optimism following years of gloom, and the impetus provided by an enlarged organisation, issued a very ambitious description of future plans. The Community was declared to have goals considerably more farreaching than simply economic collaboration. It was made clear that there should and would be attention to social problems and policies, and beyond to broad political integration. The Community was explicitly committed to achieving a "European Union" by 1980, to involve economic and monetary integration. This particular statement was notable not for reflecting a realistic appraisal of likely future developments, but rather for the generally optimistic and positive state of mind which was apparent. Special emphasis was given to regional development, a strong concern of Heath's. It was agreed that the Commission would provide staff support for development of policy on the subject. More immediately, the Community members decided to establish a regional development fund the following year, with the anticipation that it would play a leading role in the second stage of supranational co-operation and integration. But if membership in the European Community was the culmination of an exceptionally long-term effort and helped bring British foreign policy more closely in line with political realities, it did not in fact immediately result in noticeable economic or even political benefits. Indeed, the period immediately after British accession was marked by comparatively strong conflict. Although generally viewed as a supporter of the European Community, Prime Minister Heath underplayed the significance of North Sea oil discoveries to the Community as a whole. The British were unable to secure regional aid commitments on a scale considered satisfactory, primarily because of German opposition. As a result, the British representatives refused to co-operate in developing a comprehensive European energy programme.[25]

As these developments imply, the British found themselves within a Community which has experienced both successes and frustrations. There is presently, as in the past, no apparent willingness on the part of the member nations to sacrifice their independent political sovereignty to a larger European institutional structure. Consequently, there has been disillusionment of earlier hopes that a strong, independently viable political community could be formed among the Common Market states, just as there has been a fading of the general notion, popular in the late 1950s and 1960s, that an Atlantic "community" was emerging. At the same time, in a number of specific and often quite technical areas, the European Community has successfully brought about at least partial harmonisation and integration of specific national policies. To some extent, there has been co-ordination of policies in agriculture, notably in pricing and marketing. Less success has been realised in industrial and, especially, energy policy, though here too there has been consistent effort to bring the members together. Regional aid policy has also been an area of partial but impressive progress. Substantial sums are being devoted to this activity, though the member governments have been unwilling to grant true independence to supranational authorities.

Looking to the external environment of relations between the Community and other nations, there has again been partial progress. Tariffs and commercial matters are handled by the Community institutions on behalf of the members. Formal association and other economic agreements have been reached by the Community as a whole with a number of African countries, plus Greece, Turkey and Malta in Europe. More generally in foreign policy, the growing distance between the United States and Europe in the early 1970s has facilitated co-operation within the Community on important matters. Regular consultations among EEC foreign ministers has permitted the member states to unite more frequently than before behind a single foreign policy spokesman.[26]

THE COMMUNITY AND DOMESTIC POLITICS

British political parties, reflecting contemporary public opinion, the deep historical aversion to close relationships with Europe, and attitudes among their own members and activists, have not always agreed on the appropriate policy toward the Community, and this was clearly the situation in the late 1960s and early 1970s. The Liberals remained consistent in advocacy of membership, as did the Tories, though the latter possibly became somewhat more muted on the subject. Labour, recoiling from the rejection of 1967, moved back again formally to oppose membership. Wilson, after departing as Prime Minister following his government's defeat in 1970, responded to this renewed strength of Labour anti-Market sentiment by adjusting his own position, but remained basically ambiguous on the subject. Along with other party spokesmen, he became increasingly critical of the Common Market, arguing in particular that the Heath government was far too flexible and generous in the negotiating conditions being offered to the Community. After Britain joined, it was maintained that the Conservatives had rushed in, too concerned with entry to pay proper attention to the conditions under which the door was finally opened.

This draws attention to the increasing domestic importance of the Common Market, and the way in which public attitudes influenced policy development. For a long time the Community was not a highly politicised issue. As Robert Lieber's detailed analysis of the role of interest groups and parties in European policy indicates, the British only gradually made this an important subject for political debate. By the mid-1960s, powerful interest groups were attempting to influence European policy, and the question of joining had become a significant matter for public discussion. In earlier years, however, it was a much more private, less controversial subject, of great concern to Cabinet members and civil servants, less so for politicians and the public.

Public attitudes toward the Common Market shifted during the 1960s and early 1970s, though not perhaps as much as a comparatively superficial reading of public opinion poll data might indicate. Table 4.1 traces the movements of opinion over most of this period. They reveal that generally during the 1960s there was clear public support for entering the Community, though frequently only a plurality rather

TABLE 4.1: *Popular Attitudes towards the Common Market*

1. If the British government were to decide that Britain's interests would best be served by joining the European Common Market, would you approve or disapprove?

Date	Approve per cent	Disapprove per cent	Don't know per cent
August 1961	49	19	32
December 1961	53	19	28
March 1962	49	23	28
June 1962	36	30	34
September 1962	46	30	24
December 1962	37	29	34

2. If any opportunity occurs for Britain to join the Common Market, would you like to see us try or drop the idea altogether?

Date	Try to join per cent	Drop the idea per cent	Don't know per cent
February/March 1963	42	37	21
June 1963	46	25	29
September 1963	46	36	18
December 1963	42	34	24
February 1964	42	33	25
July 1964	41	37	22
November 1964	44	28	28
January 1965	48	30	22
March 1965	57	22	21

3. If the British government were to decide that Britain's interests would best be served by joining the European Common Market, would you approve or disapprove?

Date	Approve per cent	Disapprove per cent	Don't know per cent
June 1965	56	20	24
September 1965	55	15	30
December 1965	66	15	19
March 1966	68	14	18
June 1966	61	16	23
September 1966	67	13	20
December 1966	66	16	18
March 1967	57	27	16
May 1967*	49	34	17
November 1967**	44	37	19
December 1967***	36	51	13

* "The government has decided that Britain's interest would best be served by applying to join the European Common Market; do you approve or disapprove?"
** "Do you approve or disapprove of the government applying for membership in the European Common Market?"
*** "Do you think that the British government should press on with its application to join the Common Market, or should it withdraw the application?" (responses in this order)

4. Do you approve or disapprove of the government applying for membership of the European Common Market?

Date	Approve per cent	Disapprove per cent	Don't know per cent
February 1970	22	57	21
July 1970	24	55	21
October 1970	22	56	22
January 1971	22	58	20
April 1971	22	60	19
June 1971	24	60	16

5. On the facts as you know them at present, are you for or against Britain joining the Common Market?

Date	For per cent	Against per cent	Don't know per cent
July 1971	25	57	18
August 1971	39	43	17
December 1971	38	47	16
April 1972	43	43	14

(Source: Gallup Poll)

than a decisive majority was in favour. The strength of support grew in the mid-1960s, then declined after the second rebuff by de Gaulle. By the early 1970s, there was decisive opposition to the Community, despite the fact that the pro-Market Conservatives were victorious in the 1970 general election.

The opposition to the Community which had developed, combined with the fact that divisions were very sharp and feelings quite strong on both sides of the issue, led Wilson after leaving office in 1970 to declare the question should be settled "once and for all" by means of a popular referendum. Once again, he appears to have vindicated his reputation as a shrewd politician. The importance of the change from traditional policy which Community membership represents to Britain is reflected in part by the strong popular desire to participate in the decision. Opinion poll data from the period (see Table 4.2) indicate that the public mood was to some extent ambiguous, but that there was support by wide margins for a direct referendum, an unprecedented device in the context of British politics, and disagreement that parliament's collective opinion should have precedence over that of the public at large.

Soon after Labour regained power in February 1974, Prime Minister

TABLE 4.2:   *Popular Attitudes towards Resolution of the Common Market Issue*

1. If parliament voted for British entry would you then be in favour (Opinion Research Centre, 1971)

Date	Yes per cent	No per cent	Don't know per cent
June 1971	27	51	21
July 1971	45	42	13
August 1971	53	36	12

2. Now that parliament has voted in favour of Britain joining the Common Market do you think that those people against going into Europe should or should not accept Parliament's decision? (ORC October/November 1971)

Should accept	51 per cent
Should not accept	37 per cent
Don't know	12 per cent

3. If parliament votes in favour of Britain joining the Common Market and public opinion is against it which should the government follow? (ORC July 1971)

Parliament	35 per cent
Public opinion	57 per cent
Don't know	8 per cent

4. In general, do you approve or disapprove of the way the government is handling the Common Market? (Gallup Poll)

Date	Approve per cent	Disapprove per cent	Don't know per cent
October 1970	21	43	36
30 September/ 4 October 1971	27	51	22

5. Before taking their final decisions about joining the Common Market, Norway, Denmark and Ireland are each having a referendum in which all the people will be able to say whether they want to join or not. Do you think Britain should do the same or not? (National Opinion Poll, March 1972)

		Entry		Voting intention		
	All	Approve	Disapprove	Con	Lab	Lib
		per cent			per cent	
Yes	78	66	91	64	87	83
No	18	31	6	31	10	12
Don't know	4	3	3	5	3	5

Wilson and Foreign Secretary James Callaghan took steps to implement this approach. There was a lengthy process of renegotiation of British entry terms with the other Community members. The new agreement which resulted was not substantially different from the existing one, and in fact there was some domestic criticism of Wilson and Callaghan for talking tough before audiences at home while being much more accommodating when addressing the Continentals.

The referendum on the new conditions was held in June 1975, and was preceded by strong campaigns within Britain on both sides of the question. The cleavage on the Common Market cut across normal partisan lines, with supporters and opponents of the organisation represented in each of the major parties. There was a severely divisive debate within Labour ranks. Anthony Wedgwood Benn, who was already established as a spokesman for the party left wing, was the most prominent figure in the controversy. In the manner of an election campaign, he, Wilson, and others travelled the country, making speeches and answering questions before public gatherings. During the national debate preceding the referendum, drama was added by the uncertainty of public sentiment.

The referendum vote itself provided a portrait of rather consistent support for the Common Market across the country. The pro-Market majority fell below sixty-five per cent in only four of the eleven regions of the nation, and all of these suffer from especially high unemployment. Wilson's position within his party was strengthened, and that of his opponents weakened. Moreover, the referendum result appears finally to have settled the Common Market question as far as the British electorate is concerned. While specific conflicts and differences of opinion with other Community members have continued to surface, notably in the area of energy policy, and the specific economic benefits of participation in the organisation remain open to serious question and debate, it is unlikely that the basic issue of membership will again be opened in a fundamental way. The referendum was billed as an opportunity for final decision, and the electorate chose to speak in a particularly decisive manner.[27]

CONCLUSIONS

The manner in which Britain has addressed and dealt with the European Community is highly instructive and congruent with observations already made about the general functioning of British political institutions in the foreign policy field. First, in the earlier years of the Community's existence, there was a gradualism and evenness characterising the adaptation of British political institutions and policy to the new European institutions, combined with a lack of sharp public debate over the subject. The British did not adjust quickly to the formation of the EEC, and were slow to appreciate its true significance. At the same time, Macmillan's reversal of policy was announced quickly, again without great public discussion or preparation. Once more, the point is reinforced that decision-makers in the British milieu have considerable independence.

Second, over time the consequences of European Economic Community membership became much more strongly appreciated by the public, in turn resulting in considerable debate over the subject. As the 1960s wore on, there was not only increased public discussion of the matter, interest groups became much more significantly involved in trying to influence policy toward Europe. The unprecedented device of a popular referendum implies the divisions within the Labour Party on this subject, and the uncertain state of public opinion. The principal lesson, however, is that despite the complex and sensitive nature of the issue, the political system was able to absorb and resolve the controversy without suffering great instability or disruption.

Third, at a level removed from this public consideration, there was a great deal of interchange on the Common Market within the government bureaucracy. Macmillan's abrupt public decision was one very important event, which was nevertheless surrounded both before and after by important discussions within and between government departments. Even after the importance of being in the Community had been accepted, there remained a number of questions about appropriate British policy on specific issues. This perspective draws attention particularly to the role of the civil service in the entire process. Apparently, the Foreign Office was especially pivotal in first turning the Prime Minister around on Europe, then exercising effective influence within the broader civil service bureaucracy. Concerned to play a role in international affairs, professional diplomats saw in Europe an arena appropriate to a nation of reduced global power and influence. While politicians, notably in the Labour Party, switched positions more than once on the issue, the Whitehall bureaucracy went through a much more consistent and even change of attitude from opposition, to indifference, to support. This does not mean that the entire structure changed position at the same pace, led by the Foreign Office. The Treasury is frequently described as the slowest and most cautious department on the subject of Europe, though such divisions between different sections were not entirely clear or sharp. Rather, the point is that there was a general movement within the bureaucracy toward Europe, and once the basic change in attitude was accomplished it remained firm.

Related to this point, the Common Market has provided an instructive and impressive example of successful interchange, collaboration and true integration among the large number of government departments involved. The British civil service has often been noted for the flexible and informal, but very close and continuous, network of communication which characterises professional relationships. Throughout the long periods of entry negotiation, there has been effective co-operation among various interested sectors of the government bureaucracy. The basic separation between domestic and foreign sectors of the civil service has not been a serious hindrance or barrier to collaboration on policy.

The ease with which different parts of the bureaucracy mesh is shown in the manner whereby the locus of policy toward the Common Market has shifted and changed in Whitehall over the years. Alterations and structural tinkering does not appear to have broken—or even endangered—communication. Rather, the lack of problems accompanying such changes indicates the strong fraternal ties within the civil service. During the earlier approaches to the Community about membership, various structural arrangements were employed by the British. The Free Trade Area initiative was handled as a joint effort of the Foreign Office, Board of Trade and the Treasury. During the extensive negotiations with the EEC from 1961 to 1963, Heath, the chief negotiator, held the position of Lord Privy Seal, was based in the Foreign Office and supported by an interdepartmental structure of diverse representation. The Treasury played a particularly important role in the negotiations at this time. By contrast, during the Wilson approach to the EEC in the middle 1960s, the new Department of Economic Affairs was quite important. The Foreign Office continued to maintain a significant position, not least because the Foreign Secretary in this period of the Labour regime, George Brown, was clearly the second man in the party, on a par with Wilson, a highly effective minister, and a very strong advocate of Common Market entry as well.[28]

During the third and successful initiative for Common Market membership, the lead on the British side was taken by the Foreign and Commonwealth Office working in tandem with the Cabinet Office.

The former tended to be more prominent in maintaining interchange among the different national participants in the negotiations and providing support to the British delegation, the latter in managing the complex group of interdepartmental civil service committees which facilitated co-ordination and the definition of policy positions. Over time, the Cabinet Office began to play an increasingly strong role in the process. Geoffrey Rippon served as principal British negotiator with the title of Chancellor of the Duchy of Lancaster. At first he was in the Foreign and Commonwealth Office, then later moved to the Cabinet Office to work on the parliamentary legislation associated with joining the Community. There is a European Unit in the Cabinet Office, until recently under the direction of Sir Patrick Nairn, which has increasingly been the main mechanism for co-ordination of Community policy. Moreover, in late 1972 John Davies, again with the Duchy of Lancaster title, took over the general responsibility for Europe from a base in the Cabinet Office.[29]

Several lessons may be drawn from these developments within the bureaucracy. First, the British government's leaders have been strongly inclined to view European policy as more closely akin to domestic than to foreign policy, at least as the latter is normally defined. Second, there are very large domestic stakes in Common Market affairs. Many of the most important issues are in such areas as agricultural, commercial and industrial policies, and it is not surprising that a significant number of the civil servants in the British permanent delegation in Brussels are from domestic departments. Third, from the opposite direction, traditionally trained diplomats, with very generalist backgrounds and inexperience in—and often distaste for—highly technical international relations, have not been inclined to be highly assertive in Community affairs or in a very good position to do so. And again, a striking feature of the history of the British approach to the Common Market has been the way mixed delegations have been created, and positions and identities of leading personalities and departments involved have changed, without great disorder and confusion or interruption of the policy process.

Finally, in very general terms, British entry into Europe indicates very strongly that the adjustment from great power to middle power has been carried full course, that global ambitions have been given up in order to achieve a more limited, concentrated focus on influencing and participating in Europe. The long, slow withdrawal from Empire and worldwide reach, which began after the Second World War, has now been accomplished.

Topics of earlier chapters lent themselves to comparisons with the United States. Because one nation was achieving superpower status while the other was declining as a traditional great power, each has faced in very different ways the same problem of effective foreign policy organisation and co-ordination within the government, and both have confronted problems of managing a defence establishment which consumes a large part of the national budget—for all these reasons, there are extremely interesting opportunities for comparisons and contrasts. Discussion of Common Market policy, however, does not lend itself so readily to comparison with the United States. If the US is experiencing a period of foreign policy flux and uncertainty, in which post-Vietnam War caution about international involvements is combined with new Congressional assertiveness in the foreign policy field, there is nevertheless no distinctive regional solution such as the British have found in Europe. The British have overcome historical attitudes in order to accept current realities. If the Americans retreat, or at least drastically redefine foreign commitments, the likely future contours of policy are not readily apparent. This leads into the nature of the Atlantic Area relationships, and more specifically the current status of British–American ties. While it was once quite valid to describe a special relationship between these two powers, the new situation of British commitment to Europe raises questions about the present status of Atlantic relations.

5 Britain and the United States

The relationship between Britain and the United States has been a topic of special and particular attention over time for a large number of foreign policy analysts, including diplomatic historians as well as political scientists. During Britain's long period as a wide-ranging world power, the national reach and interests penetrated North America. Even after the American Revolution, there was a colonial attachment to Canada, and continuing if peripheral tension with the United States. The disagreements and disputes which constantly arose between the two countries, especially concerning treatment of ships and sailors and related maritime questions, ensured that there would be mutual awareness of one another. In addition, as the US emerged during the late nineteenth and early twentieth centuries as an international power in its own right, there was an inevitable need for the two great nations to come to terms with one another. The strength and influence of each was more than sufficient to compel the other to take notice.

Beyond normal and conventional calculation and assumptions about military and political power, there has been a great deal of understandable interest in the "special relationship" between Britain and the US. Presidents and Prime Ministers have regularly referred to the alleged unique and extraordinary, and therefore special, links connecting the two powers. The very broad compatability of domestic political institutions and cultural backdrops helps to explain the phenomenon. Such ties are often emphasised quite explicitly as an underlying basis and justification for foreign policy co-operation. Among other things, these specific references may be employed as a device to transcend particular tensions by drawing attention to more general accord. Cultural ties were Churchill's favourite rhetorical tool. In his famous 1946 speech at Fulton, Missouri, for example, in which he made reference to the emerging Cold War, he spoke of the "fraternal association of English-speaking peoples".[1]

The purpose of this chapter is to describe, analyse and evaluate the character of relationships between Britain and the United States, especially in the Atlantic Area since the Second World War. The general interchange between the two nations has already been covered in the course of describing the overall Atlantic milieu after the war, British defence policy, foreign policy organisation and other matters. The discussion which follows will build upon points made earlier in order to focus very explicitly on the character of the present relationship and the history through which it has developed. One nation was once the dominant power in the area; the other has emerged to occupy the premier position. In this, they have something in common, but the notion of special relationship implies of course considerably more.

What is the exact meaning of the term "special relationship"? In fact, it is difficult to pinpoint a precise, entirely explicit definition, but this does not mean the concept lacks meaning or importance. Rather, there is a general sense among students of Anglo-American relations that the two countries have had an unusual accord over time, which is not measured so much by treaties, or other specific agreements, as by a more general and inclusive common viewpoint and broadly shared international and foreign policy interests.

Authors who address the subject, like statesmen who include it in their rhetoric, tend at times to indulge in quite vague and exaggerated statements. Nevertheless, the dominant impression left by literature which considers the subject is that there is a broad unity of outlook between the two countries which has developed over a long period of time, and indeed is not clearly measurable from a single event or date in history. Both countries, including Britain at the height of international power, have gone to exceptional lengths to avoid war with one another. This does not mean there has been a lack of conflict and tension, only that such problems have been controlled. Herbert Nicholas describes the relationship this way, at the start of a book on the history of the Anglo-American relationship:

It is not practical to say exactly when it became an axiom of British policy that war against the United States was out of the question . . . No doubt it took possession of the public and the bureaucratic minds by degrees and almost, as it were, insensibly. It never took form as a promulgated "Doctrine"; the most lasting amities are not promulgated, they are lived, and their birth is as little a matter of record as their growth . . . the history of Anglo-American relations down to World War I could almost be written in terms of the steady spread of the idea that no disagreement justified a war between Britain and the United States.

William T. R. Fox placed emphasis on much the same elements in an analysis of relations between the countries at the close of the Second World War: "Conflicts between Great Britain and the United States have not in this century been settled by men who envisioned an ultimate resort to war. Either power may therefore, in its dealings with third states, safely leave its flanks exposed to the other."[2]

To be sure, the notion of a special relationship has hardly been accepted without question or debate on the part of either nation. There have been serious disagreements over time, and there have also been strong opponents of the proposition that the two countries should be close. Understandably, those who question the Alliance's utility have been especially prominent in Britain during the years of postwar decline. Rather, the points for this analysis are that the relationship has been stronger than the strains which have challenged it, and that questioning the validity of the close ties is one form of recognition that they exist.

HISTORICAL BACKGROUND

British–American relations began in conflict, as the colonies declared independence and fought to establish and retain their status. The achievement of independence, moreover, did not put an end to the mutual acrimony. British impressment of American seamen during the Napoleonic Wars, combined with American ambitions to annex parts of Canada, led to the war of 1812. Shorter in duration, but also more indecisive, than the first war, the clash added to the existing bitterness. The British burned Washington, in a gesture which underlined American weakness and became symbolic of the intensity of ill-feeling between the two countries.

Without doubt, these early conflicts were considerably more significant to the Americans than the British. The United States was very secondary to the Britain which was engaged in a continuing struggle for survival with Napoleon's France. Even after Waterloo, the other great powers of Europe understandably remained much more important to British foreign policy than the new, distant and comparatively weak nation in North America.

Nevertheless, it was rather quickly apparent that the Americans would occupy a larger amount of British attention. The British had interests in Latin America as well as Canada, and questions of the role of colonial powers in that part of the world brought them into contact with the US. Again, it is important to note that the result was far from being clear opposition between the two nations. Just before the declaration of the Monroe Doctrine in 1823, for example, British Foreign Secretary Canning and Richard Rush of the US came very close to an accord on a public declaration favouring independence for Spanish colonies in Latin America. When the Monroe Doctrine was actually announced by the American President at the end of the year, there was no great concern or even attention on the part of the European powers; though the declaration would be important to American diplomacy in the future, the significant development at the time was a demand by the British, directed at France, that trade with Spanish colonies must not be hampered, outside powers must not intervene in Latin American independence struggles, and the United States must be included in any discussions of Latin American affairs among Europeans. British naval power in effect enforced the Doctrine which the Americans were too weak to defend sufficiently. Latin America continued to be an area where Anglo-American interests merged, or at least crossed paths, notably in the controversial Clayton–Bulwer Treaty of 1850. More generally, the two nations were involved in boundary disputes concerning Canada, with two comprehensive settlements reached in the 1840s.[3]

The American Civil War drew even further British attention. The basic strategic lessons of the conflict, in particular the effect of trench warfare, combined with devastating firepower, in producing stalemate and very high casualties, were not absorbed by the Europeans, who were in consequence shocked at developments after the outbreak of the First World War. On the other hand, the political dimensions of the Civil War were of considerable interest in Britain. There was a great deal of sympathy for the Confederacy, centred in but not limited to the traditional English aristocracy. Using the most transparent formal subterfuge, Confederate warships, including the notorious *Alabama*, were built in British shipyards. In consequence, there was some real danger after the end of the war that the Union armies— large, well-armed and just victorious—might successfully invade Canada. Ultimately, these fears failed to materialise; but relations between the two countries did not begin to improve until the *Alabama* claims were settled and the Treaty of Washington signed in 1871. The treaty established rules for arbitration of disputes and settled various maritime quarrels. The arbitration which followed provided the US with $15,500,000 in settlement for the losses suffered because of actions of Confederate ships built in Britain. Again, the British had a strong incentive to deal with the Americans because of the course of events in Europe, specifically the Franco-Prussian War and the Russian abrogation of the neutrality of the Black Sea.[4]

Beyond concerns related to the Civil War, the British were beginning to take more general notice of the emerging Republic across the Atlantic. The United States might not yet rival the greatest military powers of Europe, and distance reinforced this point to weaken the incentive of policy planners in European capitals to pay close attention. At the same time, the US was moving to occupy a position of considerable economic consequence to Britain, especially as the centre of large amounts of invested capital. There was also British interest in, if not admiration for, the American political system. British political institutions were generally regarded as superior, of course, with this sentiment—as already noted—shared widely on the other side of the Atlantic; but this did not mean others were completely ignored. Walter Bagehot, in his classic *The English Constitution*, devotes sharp and incisive attention to the US in a brilliant comparative analysis of structures and styles of governing. His classic essay stands alone in several respects, but also represents a broader British interest in the institutions of the new Republic.[5]

As the nineteenth century wore on, both nations began to converge, not in formal alliance, but rather in the more general perception that they had an interest in avoiding an armed conflict with one another. There were no formal alliances; but, more informally, the US and Britain saw that there was a broad area where their interests combined and merged. The Americans were secure in their isolation, the British in their unchallenged naval power. As the new nation grew in economic influence and military strength, the established great power found even more cause to pay heed.

There were specific disputes between the two countries, but none so important that it overcame this general environment of amity and concord. The Americans became increasingly protectionist, an important cause of strain in light of British trading interests in the US. The 1890 McKinley Tariff was particularly galling to the British, since it had a strong impact on several kinds of principal manufactured goods. There were continuing maritime conflicts between the US and Canada, and disagreements about the Alaskan boundary. There was pressure in the US to build a national canal in Panama, even though this would violate the provisions of the 1850 Clayton–Bulwer Treaty with the British. There was a border dispute between British Guiana and Venezuela, which threatened to bring British military intervention, in violation of the Monroe Doctrine. Farther away geographically from the United States, but perhaps most important of all in impact on domestic politics, the conflict between Ireland and England created a strong and continuing reaction in the Unites States among influential ethnic groups opposed to British government policy.

Most of these issues were settled during the last decade of the nineteenth century and the first of the twentieth century. Arbitration was used for a number of them, and a 1912 treaty, in the wake of a dispute over Newfoundland, provided for permanent mechanisms to handle such difficulties in the future.[6]

Most serious of all the problems during the period was the Venezuelan boundary dispute. Following the failure of a number of attempts at negotiated settlement, President Cleveland's Administration in 1895 escalated tensions by formally accusing the British of violating the Monroe Doctrine and threatening war. The British, not surprisingly under the circumstances, handled the note in a manner which further increased growing American anger. There was a long, purposeful delay in the British response. The reply, when it came, amounted to a rejection of the American position. In return, the US insisted on arbitration, and the two nations, without explicitly wanting to do so, seemed to be moving steadily and surely toward armed conflict over the question.

Eventually, however, the British began to back away from confrontation, and the Americans followed suit. Arbitration was accepted, and the final settlement was generally in line with the Venezuelan position, though American pressure was required to get that nation to accept it. The British were aware that the relatively stable European system of international relations was gradually disintegrating; in consequence, there was a desire to maintain an amicable tone with the Americans. In 1902, there was another retreat from Venezuela, following expressions of American concern over British and German military moves in reaction to failure to pay debts. Generally in Latin America, the British were careful to avoid offending American concerns and interests.[7]

In other areas as well, the two powers found they had a good deal in common. The British were not concerned by American expansion in the Pacific, including the taking of the Philippines and Hawaii. They refused aid to Spain in the brief war with the US in 1898. In the Far East, the two powers collaborated in promoting an "open door" policy whereby the freedom of both to intervene in the economic affairs of China and other nations would be preserved.

There are several lessons which emerge from this consideration of nineteenth-century relations between Britain and the US. First, while much has been made in recent years about a special positive relationship between the two, the fact remains that there was considerable conflict, not only at the start of the relationship, but also rather continuously over time. Second, however, there was also a growing trend toward common interests, in which conflict was not allowed to overcome a more basic desire to co-operate. In the first part of the century, general hostility, and the specific issue of British impressment of American seamen, was sufficient to lead to war. However, while the domestic divisions and strains within the United States during the Civil War were unprecedented, even on the Union side alone, there was still no outbreak of hostilities with Britain, even after the surrender of the Confederacy in 1865. Similarly, disagreements over Latin America, despite the fact that Britain was a world power and the United States had formally declared a special interest in that area, did not lead to war.

The unsuccessful effort to avoid war on the part of the two countries reflected various general interests. The British did not view the United States as sufficiently close, hostile or powerful to pose a serious military threat. At the same time, British leaders were sensitive to the fact that relations among European nations were gradually deteriorating, and in particular that Germany was posing a growing direct military threat. There was no predicting the holocaust to come, but there was clear perception of approaching dangers and possible war. Moreover, the United States was an important market for British goods and capital. On the American side, the sense of national destiny might create continuing tensions with Canada, and occasional problems with Britain, but was not sufficient to lead to a direct challenge to British military power.

More generally still, despite a history of conflict, there was also broad cultural compatability between the two nations. Britain, especially in the nineteenth century, might not have been a democracy in American terms, but did have an established tradition of popular representation in the institutions of government which contrasted with the other great powers of Europe. There might be important social differences between the two countries, but at the same time British cultural styles were influential in the US, particularly in certain areas such as the character of higher education among elite colleges and universities.

In summary, tensions did not lead to warfare after 1812, and were mitigated by a strong sense of common interests. Moreover, true to their general style, the British were able to employ flexibility and adaptability in relations with the Americans, as with others. Growing American economic and military power was accommodated rather than resisted, especially since the new nation was far removed, literally and figuratively, from the central diplomatic arena of Europe.

These general qualities of Anglo-American relations, and especially the British capacity to adjust to changing circumstances, continued during the twentieth century. As American power grew to parallel, and finally surpass, the British, there was an acceptance of these new restrictions. Broad agreement on principles, especially from the start of American intervention in the Second World War, and the irrefutable and pressing need to collaborate, kept the two sides together despite specific, and at times quite important, policy and strategy conflicts.

THE TWO WORLD WARS

When it broke out in 1914, the First World War was expected by virtually all the participants to be a comparatively brief conflict; the disillusionment came quickly. Soon, the armies of Europe were bogged down in enormously costly stalemate. It is important to keep in mind that the sympathy with the Allied cause which was apparent from the start in the United States during the Second World War was *not* present at the beginning of the First World War. Ethnic immigrant groups from both sides in the First World War were represented in American politics, and while there was strong sympathy for Britain and the Allied side, no clear consensus developed for actually entering the war until the Germans commenced unrestricted submarine warfare in 1917.

The British followed a policy of astute restraint concerning limitation of trade with enemy nations. There was, as in previous conflicts with Continental powers, an effort to blockade, which was the British analogue to submarine warfare. There was also, however, considerable caution in actually imposing the blockade. It was realised that there was an important need not to alienate the US, especially in view of the economic recession then in progress, by abruptly cutting off trade with the Continent. Therefore, the blockade was not imposed until after the US had developed a vigorous trade with the Allies. As the British Foreign Secretary, Edward Grey, stated in his memoirs: "It was better . . . to carry on the war without blockade . . . than to incur a break with the United States . . . The object of diplomacy, therefore, was to secure the maximum of blockade that could be enforced without a rupture with the United States." British restraint ultimately was rewarded when the US intervened on the Allied side in 1917, just in time to blunt and turn back the last great German offensive of the war.[8]

The interwar period was marked by some serious problems and disagreements between the two nations, but also by significant accords. The latter occurred notably in the area of naval strength. Recognising the new reality that the United States had become a leading world naval power, Britain was willing, at the Washington naval conference of 1922, to accept parity in large capital ships, while the Japanese, French and Italians agreed to levels of strength below that of the two primary powers. The treaty also involved a freeze on ship construction. These conditions were extended and expanded at the London naval conference of 1930, though the new accords broke down six years later. There were tensions over the payment of war debts, a problem which affected European–American relations generally during this period. The British position in particular was not helped by a note from the Treasury to the US government in 1932, stating baldly that it would be better for all concerned if the debts went unpaid.[9]

The Second World War brought much less ambiguity for the United States concerning which side to support. Well before Pearl Harbour, President Roosevelt was employing American resources to aid the British and manoeuvring to increase the commitment. The neutrality laws governing US conduct at the time were reinterpreted to permit large amounts of arms aid to Britain and Canada, including the sale of fifty over-age US destroyers for naval bases in the Atlantic and Caribbean. The Lend-Lease Act gave the President very great freedom in aiding foreign countries in the interest of protecting the security of the US.

The actual formal entrance of the United States into the war as a combatant brought even more collaboration with the British. Churchill and Roosevelt were inevitably closer than was either with Stalin, the third partner in the Alliance. Also, there was below this highest level considerable co-operation among military officers from the two countries.

There were also frictions, however, both during and after the war. The American cancellation of Lend-Lease and conditions for economic aid were one aspect. There was also the breakdown of atomic weapons collaboration, a topic already mentioned in the general context of British defence policy. Both of the nations had researchers working on problems of atomic power development when the war broke out. At first, the British were not strongly interested in collaboration. By 1942, however, policy had changed to favour integration of the atomic effort with that of the Americans. During this difficult part of the war, after the US had entered but while the Axis still retained considerable military initiative, the two nations were drawing more closely together in general co-operation. Also, the British sensed that the enormous technological capacity of the ally was greater than their own. With farsightedness, it was realised in British policy circles that atomic weapons would be a most important post-war factor. As Andrew Pierre notes in his comprehensive study of British nuclear policy:

> In retrospect, the determined, sometimes desperate British effort to continue to have a significant role in the creation of the first atomic bomb stemmed from an awareness of the effect that nuclear weapons would have upon world politics. That nuclear weapons would be an important index of strength for a Great Power in the post-war pecking order was seen, if perhaps only hazily, by the leaders of a nation that had long been accustomed to being on top. [10]

The size of the atomic development effort which the Americans were able to mount resulted in the project being clearly centred in that country. In 1942 Churchill, very much aware of British vulnerability to German attack, actually made the suggestion to Roosevelt that the atomic project be located in the US; had the Americans not agreed, the British would have gone to the Canadians with the request. In the event, Roosevelt fully concurred that the operation should be centred in one country, with close collaboration between the two allies.

Once the project was underway, however, there were problems of British access to materials and information. The agreement to co-operate made by Churchill and Roosevelt was most informal; in fact, it was not even written down. Lacking binding restrictions, the American military, characteristically security conscious, cut off information from the British ally. This in turn resulted in protests from

Churchill, and in a specific written agreement, signed at the Quebec meeting of the late summer of 1943. This formalized co-operation among the US, Britain and Canada in atomic weapon development. In keeping with Roosevelt's style of operation, the accord was kept very secret, with neither Congress nor Vice-President Truman being informed. [11]

POSTWAR POLICY UNTIL 1956

After the war, the lack of understanding surrounding Anglo-American atomic co-operation resulted in serious conflict, as we have seen. The problem was not just the secrecy of the Quebec agreement; there was strong resistance in the US, centred in the Congress, to any information-sharing. There were efforts by the new Truman and Attlee governments to reach a fresh understanding, but these were overcome by passage of the McMahon Act in 1946. Learning about the Quebec accords strengthened rather than weakened Congressional determination to keep atomic secrets and materials in American hands. The fact that Britain was a source of uranium also created resentment; the 1947 agreement for limited co-operation in this area was undertaken only because of ore shortages in the US. Truman made tentative efforts to revive the more general wartime collaboration, but the opposition of powerful Congressional leaders, including Senator Vandenberg, ensured that these would fail. The growth of intense concern about security in the US, the rise of Senator McCarthy, the prosecution of Klaus Fuchs in Britain for treason in providing nuclear secrets to the Soviet Union, and the awesome power of the new weapons themselves, were all doubtless factors which influenced the American attitude. In terms of Britain, the situation meant that atomic capacity had to be developed independently of the Americans. At enormous financial cost, the British pressed ahead with nuclear development. [12]

Gradually, American policy on sharing information with the British turned more liberal as the atmosphere of the Cold War became an accepted part of the international *status quo* and Senator McCarthy's impact and influence declined. Modification of the McMahon Act permitted co-operation on military uses of atomic energy. Nevertheless, the important point remains that, despite the prominence of the notion of a "special relationship" on both sides of the Atlantic, the US was in fact quite suspicious and reluctant concerning actual sharing of information with Britain. Equally important, the British were able to contain the hostility engendered by American policy. To be sure, there was bitterness; but—as in the realm of economic affairs—in nuclear matters British leaders did not allow this to damage the continuing alliance with the Americans. They were able to serve, despite a shrinking economic base, as a catalyst to bring the US and Europe together in alliance after the war. Interest in maintaining especially close collaboration with the Americans remained high.

SUEZ AND AFTER

The Suez disaster returns again and again to confront consideration of British foreign policy since the Second World War. The event is important from several analytical perspectives, but perhaps most of all in the context of Anglo-American relations. It was, after all, the resistance of the Eisenhower Administration to the British–French initiative which doomed the invasion from the start. The British were hamstrung by the fragile economic position of the nation; moreover, the operation itself highlighted the limitations of British and French military capabilities. It is not surprising, therefore, that the adventure was followed by a comprehensive review of defence policy, with the result that substantial reductions were undertaken to bring commitments more in line with economic restraints.

Suez was important from the perspective of British foreign policy generally, in that the misadventure underlined the fact that the nation was no longer a great power; it was also significant from the more limited viewpoint of the Anglo-American partnership. It was shown that a comparatively minor exercise of American influence and leverage could have enormous, indeed decisive, consequences for Britain. Perhaps not since before the Second World War had the relationship been truly one of equals; moreover, for a long period before that war it was apparent that one nation was expanding tremendously in power and influence while the other was gradually losing ground to industrial and military competitors. Nevertheless, before Suez there was no broad appreciation of how disparate the two partners really had become.

Related to this fundamental point, Suez indicates that, despite the closeness of the alliance and the good personal relations between certain American and British leaders, there were still possibilities for great miscalculation and error. It is important to note that Eisenhower and Dulles did not have a close rapport, or even apparently a good working relationship, with Prime Minister Eden. Nevertheless, Suez represents a miscalculation by the British of truly enormous proportions. Obviously, it was assumed throughout the planning of the military operation that the United States would accept the Anglo-French action. Just as clearly, Dulles and Eisenhower had no intention of doing so. Part of the explanation, as noted earlier, is that the regular Foreign Office and broader foreign policy channels within the Whitehall professional civil service were not consulted by Eden and those closest to him who did the planning. Rather, atypically for the British, the decision was made by a very small, private circle of leaders at the very top. In this basic sense, Suez was very much Eden's own personal initiative. The broader point, however, remains: though there might be a special relationship between Britain and the US, understanding was not sufficient to prevent—or even warn of—disastrous misperception.

The lesson of Suez, in terms of the relationship with the United States, was taken to heart by the British. Following Suez, the British never again engaged in a major departure in foreign policy without first consulting carefully with the United States. If it had been shown that Britain could no longer operate with the freedom of earlier periods, with this disaster there was also appreciation of, and adjustment to, new realities. The policy failure not only brought a new Prime Minister, Harold Macmillan, to power, it also brought recognition at last of altered national status and position in the international system.

Suez did not mean, however, that there was no meaning left to the special relationship between the two nations. Quite the contrary was the case. In reaction to Suez on the American side, there was increased willingness to try to restore amicable relations with Great Britain. President Eisenhower, for instance, was accommodating to Britain in amending the McMahon Act to permit free sharing of nuclear military information. On the other side, Macmillan gave improved relations with the United States the highest priority. He and Eisenhower had worked together during the Second World War, and in the circumstances of the late 1950s effectively re-established their earlier personal accord. In 1958, the British and Americans collaborated very closely in handling a crisis situation in the Middle East. Following a coup in Iraq, the nation moved from a pro-Western position to one much more sympathetic to the Soviet Union. Leaders in Jordan and Lebanon, concerned about infiltration of men and arms over the border from Iraq, requested American and British intervention.

United States marines and an army brigade were sent to Lebanon, and American planes were used to transport a British paratroop regiment to Jordan. The crisis passed without outbreak of war, and the effective collaboration among the civilian leadership and military organisations of the two nations did a great deal to improve relations.[13]

In general, the end of the Eisenhower Administration marked an upgrade in international understanding between Britain and the US. The frictions, personal as well as policy-linked, of the Eden period were over. Macmillan showed a facility for getting along with the Americans which his predecessor had lacked.

This new effectiveness of British policy in the Atlantic Area meant, among other things, that the American habit of relying strongly on the West Germans lost some momentum. American favouritism toward this ally reflected a combination of concern and confidence about central European security. There was continual fear that the Germans would somehow be drawn into the Eastern orbit, most likely through a Soviet ploy which appealed to the strong German desire for national reunification. Hence, there was an incentive to try to bind West Germany as firmly as possible to the NATO Alliance and the rest of West Germany. There was also appreciation for the reliable anti-Communism of Adenauer and his Christian Democratic Party; unlike British Tories, they had no clouded past of attempted appeasement of totalitarian aggressors. More concretely, the West Germans were willing to make a very substantial military contribution to NATO. Finally, Dulles himself was strongly pro-German. The new British finesse, however, combined with the death of Dulles, meant that the German–American tie was no longer quite so close and exclusive. Eisenhower's more direct involvement in the details of diplomacy near the end of his Administration meant, on balance, that Washington attitudes were more strongly pro-British and less pro-German than before.

Eisenhower's friendliness to British concerns was very explicitly apparent in the willingness to commit the US to provide the Skybolt missile to maintain the credibility of the British bomber force. Rising costs of missile development, combined with the failure of the Blue Streak to reach the deployment stage, moved the British to search for ways to maintain the deterrent in the future. This, in turn, created a focus on the American Skybolt, which promised to keep bombers from becoming obsolete by transforming them into platforms for launching missiles. Eisenhower's commitment to Macmillan was strong but informal, given in a personal way toward the end of his tenure in office.

It meant, ultimately, that while relations between the two countries were generally improving, a specific problem was looming which would considerably complicate matters in the future.[14]

THE 1960s: KENNEDY AND ATLANTICISM

The early 1960s brought a new Administration to power in Washington which was strongly motivated to follow a more assertive and vigorous foreign policy than the Eisenhower Administration, and to make relationships with European allies more explicit by basing them on clearer policy understandings. President Kennedy and his chief advisers were keenly interested in European affairs; a number of them had backgrounds associated with the postwar period of American aid and commitment to the defence of the region. The change in leadership in Washington meant, more specifically, that changes were made in the approach to important diplomatic and military issues.

The new Administration was anxious to establish more precision and rationality in nuclear weapons policy through substitution of the doctrine of flexible response for massive retaliation. In the 1950s, the Eisenhower Administration had been formally committed to the stance that even very limited encroachments by the Communist *bloc* nations would be met by the full nuclear retaliatory capacity of the US. Strongly reflecting a concern with economy, a personal disposition of the President's as well as a characteristic Republican Party attitude, the policy was viable as long as the Soviet nuclear arsenal was modest. As the other side developed a significant bomber and—later—missile capability, the policy became less credible and pressures grew for modification. Responding to the new situation, President Kennedy and his advisers were anxious to bring policy in line with changed circumstances. The defence budget was increased to support a wider range of policy options and capabilities. Both strategic nuclear and other conventional forces were built up.

This, in turn, brought a reaction of some suspicion on the part of the European allies. During the Eisenhower Administration, there had been insecurity that Europe might be devastated as part of a general nuclear exchange over which they had no control. Now, especially since the new regime in Washington was also firmly on the record against European nations developing their own nuclear forces, many NATO allies worried that the situation was becoming even more undesirable. The emphasis on conventional forces raised fears that war in Europe might become more likely. Connected to this, pressures on the Europeans to boost their own conventional forces fostered resentment; the situation seemed to be turning into one where the Americans wanted to restrict their collaborators to the role of "infantry" while they retained the status of nuclear "cavalry" for themselves. From the perspectives of domestic political constraints, military calculations and responses, and the inevitable power differential between themselves and the US, West Europeans were given pause by an American approach which seemed to create at least as many problems as were solved.

From a much broader political and diplomatic viewpoint, the Kennedy Administration was also extremely active in promoting co-operation and a form of integration among the Atlantic Area nations. For years, there had been general interest in informed circles, including and going beyond policy-makers, in developing close ties among these countries. Governor Nelson Rockefeller, among other prominent political leaders, had been active in promoting such conceptions. The new Administration picked up the notion and gave it considerable impetus, though not more explicit conceptual definition. The President, in a widely publicised speech in Philadelphia on 4 July 1962, spoke about an emerging Atlantic community of nations which would guide international affairs generally in the future. Again, the fact that this was a very broad conception, with a lack of clear steps or a precise plan of procedure, gave some observers pause. Moreover, the American emphasis on partnership and equality was out of tune with the policy of US command and control in nuclear matters. At the same time that the President was describing the need to build a fair and equitable Atlantic partnership, his Secretary of Defense, Robert McNamara, was focusing on the need to maintain strategic military initiative in American hands.[15]

For various reasons, the new Administration was considerably less jarring and troubling for the British than the other principal West European nations. Britain was clearly a member of the nuclear club, and this had been explicitly recognised by the US in the reform of the McMahon Act in 1958. Thanks to this pact, Britain, in contrast to some other European nations, in particular France under de Gaulle, was favourably disposed to much greater American involvement in European affairs. It is true that the British, like the French, were not supportive of far-reaching political integration among the nations of the European Economic Community, a policy favoured by the US; but this difference did not seriously endanger Anglo-American relations, especially since Britain was not a member of the Community and the goal of political unity seemed still to be quite far away.

Finally, on a more personal level, Prime Minister Macmillan was able, apparently somewhat to his surprise, to establish an especially close rapport with the new American President. Chancellor Adenauer in West Germany had been highly effective in dealing with Eisenhower and Dulles. The American leaders were, like others in NATO, concerned throughout the 1950s about the two intertwined topics of ensuring West German loyalty to the broader Atlantic community, and the potential menace represented by growing German military power. While the US had been a strong supporter of German rearmament, there was no doubt about the potential dangers of military resurgence in that nation. Beyond the requirements of foreign policy, there was, as noted above, a personal congeniality between the American leaders and the German Chancellor, with the overall result that West Germany was an influential Alliance partner, even though— and in part because—it was a source of worry to Americans and Europeans alike.

The Kennedy Administration, on the other hand, brought to power a number of high-level policy-makers who, in temperament as well as age, seemed out of tune with the very senior German leader. Macmillan as well was concerned about the new government in Washington; he was so much older than the new President that it was natural to worry that he would not have the rapport that had been established with Eisenhower. Their first encounter in Washington had been a bland, formal discussion, not a great success on the personal level. This proved, however, to be an atypical meeting. Following the conclusion of the acrimonious Vienna Summit with Khrushchev in the spring of 1961, the President called on Macmillan in London. After the stresses and tensions of the confrontation with the Soviet Premier, Kennedy seemed very glad to be seeing an ally. The meeting with Macmillan proved to be a tonic, laying the basis for a close friendship which continued until Kennedy's assassination. The talk in London was relaxed; any semblance of formal agenda was abandoned. The two leaders discovered that while they were separated by a wide gap in terms of years, in temperament and taste there was remarkable similarity. Kennedy consulted often with Macmillan, especially during very serious situations, including the Cuban Missile Crisis. When Kennedy was assassinated the following year, the Prime Minister's statement of eulogy was singular among the many expressed by national leaders around the world, being particularly and uncharacteristically emotional.

In more specific and formal terms, Anglo-American relations were eased by the British decision to seek Common Market entry in 1961. Since the Community's earliest days, reaching back to the preliminary organisations set up during the period right after the Second World War, the Americans had been supporters of integration. British foreign policy in this important area was, therefore, brought more in line with the US, whether or not there was quick success in gaining entry.

The friendship between Kennedy and Macmillan, and the growing similarity in important aspects of policy, did not mean there were no serious policy problems between the two countries during this period. The lessons and effects of Suez had been absorbed, and the Americans were anxious to repair the divisions which had been created. At the same time, the very fact of dependence and dominance—in other words, the significant differential in sheer power—meant that tensions were endemic to the relationship and problems very difficult to avoid.

This point was brought home forcefully by the Skybolt crisis of 1962. This generally is regarded as one of the very few most serious policy conflicts between the British and Americans in the postwar period. While, unlike Suez, the Skybolt affair did not involve military operations, the two events are linked in the sense that both resulted from truly enormous misperceptions and miscalculations between the two countries. These were two nations, moreover, which were formally allied and informally in close contact, with a long history of collaboration and interchange. Both crises indicate that the special relationship, even if important, is not sensitive enough to prevent such serious misunderstandings.

The British came to Skybolt through default, and once focused upon the weapon became the centre of hopes to maintain a national deterrent. Other systems, notably Blue Streak, were too expensive, too quickly obsolete, or simply totally beyond the capacity of a straitened economy. Skybolt, on the other hand, would extend the life of bombers already in being. The fact that the missile would be integrated with bombers was especially appealing to air force officers who wanted to preserve the romance and adventure of manned flight. Along this line, naval officers were aware that the principal alternative to Skybolt was the Polaris missile, and equally did not want to sacrifice a surface blue-water capacity to concentrate on submarines. Aside from cost considerations, the new technology presented the possibility of a much less exciting existence.

The new American Administration which took office in 1961, however, did not feel compelled to honour the British request for Skybolt. After all, Eisenhower had not formalised his understanding with Macmillan, which remained very personal and outside the boundaries of explicit policy commitment. Kennedy and his advisers were interested primarily in a comprehensive re-evaluation and reorganisation of defence policy. Strategically, the Administration was guided by the belief that the deterrent should be as well protected and stable as possible. In practical terms, this resulted in a de-emphasis on bombers in favour of strategic missiles, especially of the long-range variety which could be placed in hardened silos in the US and in submarines. The new Secretary of Defense was confronted with a whole range of development and procurement decisions, under the general rubric of the new strategy. One general result of this situation was that the Skybolt missile appeared increasingly to be of use only to the British defence effort, and not at all closely related to the American. Moreover, the system had become of overriding concern to the British, while of only peripheral importance among a range of American policy considerations and decisions.[16]

There was a further complication in that final decisions on Skybolt were made by the Kennedy Administration very soon after the Cuban Missile Crisis of 1962. The two subjects are not inherently related, but the coincidence of timing and scheduling meant that one had a strong bearing on the other. The President's chief subordinates were in a relaxed and confident mood following the resolution of this most direct and dramatic nuclear confrontation; not surprisingly in view of the fact that they had come so close to the brink of nuclear holocaust without stepping or being pushed over. They were not, therefore, especially attuned to the likelihood of further serious problems of a different order, this time involving the principal ally rather than the most powerful opponent. Also, the Cuban Missile Crisis was enormously preoccupying in terms of the dangers of general war and the consequent pressures on top-level decision-makers. As a result, other decisions pressing at this time were often made very quickly, pushed aside until later, and not approached with the customary careful staff review.

These factors help to explain the abrupt manner in which Skybolt was cancelled by Secretary of Defense McNamara in late 1962. The overriding evidence for him was economic and budgetary: the weapon was simply not cost-effective. British needs and sensitivities were not weighted in the calculus. There was apparently a problem of incomprehension by each side of the problems, limitations and concerns of the other. The Americans assumed the British would find a way out of the crisis, perhaps by asking for the new Polaris submarine missile. The British could not really believe Skybolt would be cancelled, and if the unexpected actually happened there was apparently an assumption that Polaris would be offered automatically.

In fact, McNamara had considered the possibility of offering the Polaris missile to the British, but was strenuously opposed by the State Department. Pentagon officials were principally concerned with coherence and efficiency in weapons policy. In the State Department, however, the likely diplomatic repercussions of what was suggested carried considerable weight. There, worries about proliferation and broad international consistency in policy, and in particular the predictable reaction of de Gaulle to special consideration for the British, were paramount. This State Department resistance, in turn, led McNamara to pull back from the Polaris option.

The magnitude of the misunderstanding which followed reportedly startled and puzzled President Kennedy. After all, his personal relationship with Macmillan could not have been better, and the Administration had no shortage of officials highly sophisticated in Atlantic relations. If the British were counting so heavily on Skybolt, why had this point not been made far more forcefully to Washington? To get a clearer picture of how the problem could have become so large and threatening, in such a surprising manner, the President commissioned Richard Neustadt, the political scientist whose influential studies on presidential power had impressed him, to undertake a thorough review of events and developments related to the communications breakdown.

Meanwhile, there was an immediate pressing crisis to resolve, which Kennedy and Macmillan did at the Nassau conference of December 1962. The discussions were intensive and not entirely friendly. The British pressed very hard to save Skybolt for their air force. Only when this proved impossible was there acquiescence to the American offer of Polaris missiles. There had been a suggestion that the less sophisticated, shorter range variant of Skybolt, titled Hound Dog, might be offered the British; but the point was made—publicly by English journalist Henry Brandon—that it would be highly inappropriate to try and base British independence on a missile with such a name.[17]

The reverberations from the Skybolt affair were quite significant. Despite the closeness of the Anglo-American relationship, it was shown that each nation could have not only very different policy priorities, but also sharply contrasting perceptions of the same situation. De Gaulle very likely would have vetoed British membership in the Common Market the following year no matter what had transpired; but the Skybolt crisis provided very hard evidence that the special relationship between the Anglo-Saxons, if it could not prevent problems, did facilitate nuclear solutions of the sort which the Americans were willing to offer no other country. There had, in fact, been an Anglo-American rebuff to de Gaulle's suggestion in 1958 to establish a three-way nuclear directorate to manage the Alliance. Nassau showed that a special relationship did exist, however ambiguous in practice; this notion, often discussed with scepticism by observers in the two countries, was clearly accepted as reality by de Gaulle in his veto.

The rest of the 1960s did not contain a crisis in Anglo-American relations comparable to Skybolt; rather, the two countries seemed to travel along increasingly divergent policy paths. The British drew back steadily from pretentions to broad world influence, including the military dimensions of such a role. The Americans moved ever more deeply into Vietnam, distracting attention and military resources to Asia, away from Europe. European allies might have chosen to join the Americans in the Indochina war; Johnson Administration spokesmen, notably Secretary of State Dean Rusk, very frequently urged that this be done. It was not; domestic political restrictions, combined with different strategic calculations about the importance of Indochina, militated against participating in the American adventure.

For Britain, moving to a more reduced status need not have necessarily endangered close ties with the US; looking to Europe might have included an Atlantic perspective as well, with commensurate reinforcement of the American link. After all, successive Administrations in Washington had been strongly supportive of the European Community, to include Britain as a full member. Again, however, the US was turning away from close involvement with European affairs. In view of American preoccupation elsewhere, the British found that their own growing focus on Europe put distance between themselves and the US.[18]

Britain, to be sure, still retained ambitions for influence which travelled well beyond the confines of Europe, but here too the problem of Vietnam created frictions between the two allies. Prime Minister Wilson made several attempts to intervene to end, or at least de-escalate, the war in Vietnam. In each instance, there was failure and often considerable American irritation. Several missions were sent between 1964 and 1966 to try to assist in drawing the conflict to a close; all were failures. Once again, Britain was attempting to act as a mediator between East and West, but the decline of national influence had gone further than in earlier years, when Macmillan had been trying to ease Cold War tensions.

The late 1960s and early 1970s brought changes of leadership in both London and Washington; but with no very significant departures in the relationship between the two nations. Nixon and Heath apparently had a reasonably good mutual understanding; there were some parallels in their careers, and Heath had been cordial to Nixon during the latter's period out of power before 1968. There was not, however, the same personal warmth which existed between Kennedy or Eisenhower and Macmillan. More generally, there was not the same sort of steady and regular consultation over time which characterised interchange among national leaders in earlier periods. The US might still be of very great consequence to Britain, but the reverse did not necessarily apply.

Secretary of State Henry Kissinger's declaration of 1973 to be the Year of Europe created problems for the special relationship as it did for Atlantic relations generally. The statement followed a period when Britain, along with the rest of Europe, had been alienated by harsh criticism from both Kissinger and President Nixon, especially during a period of very close American contact with the Soviet Union. Also, at this time Heath and other European leaders were trying to work out a statement of goals and purposes for the European Economic Community; the American initiative drew attention implicitly to the tensions which had developed in Atlantic relations, and at the same time underlined the ambiguity for a Britain which gave primary importance both to the American tie and Community membership. Because the British were late in joining Europe, and not wholehearted even after they had entered, the problems between the two sides of the Atlantic carried special significance for them.

This was followed by the sharp differences between the US and important Western European allies over the Middle East war of 1973. The US commitment to Israel, reflected by the sudden emergency alert of American armed forces around the world and the airlift of military aid, contrasted with the more reticent positions of Western European nations, including Britain. The West Germans complained about use of their ports by American ships supplying Israel; the British were reported to have been unwilling to permit US planes to use bases in Cyprus. With irony, then, the year which was supposedly to be devoted to improvement of European–American understanding concluded with an especially strong division between the two sides of the Atlantic.[19]

It was on this low note that the Labour Party returned to power in 1974, and took steps to improve Anglo-American relations. Specifically, Foreign Secretary Callaghan and Kissinger began an informal, but concentrated and extensive, series of talks, aimed at bettering Alliance relations generally and in particular the understanding between the two countries. While no specific formal agreement resulted from the interchange, there is general consensus on the observation that the talks did contribute directly to an improvement in the overall diplomatic atmosphere, and to personal goodwill between the two officials.

CONCLUSIONS

It is particularly appropriate to discuss the special relationship between Britain and the US in the long term, for understanding and mutual interest, if not close co-operation on an explicit basis, reach back comparatively far in time. From the earliest period in US history, following the achievement of independence and the resolution of the most severe conflicts with Britain, there has been a realisation that the two countries have large incentives for avoiding war with one another. The Americans at any rate for a long time could do little to challenge British power; the British, with characteristic flexibility, overcame animosity to the new country and saw the advantages to be gained by coexistence. Once again, British foreign policy has remained generally consistent over a long period of time; once again, the early history of Anglo-American relations provides evidence of British willingness to adapt to new and different circumstances.

As American power increased, the incentives for accord were correspondingly greater. Economic investment in the new country was a factor of steadily growing significance. American assistance in two world wars, and especially in the second conflict, cemented the bonds of emotion and political necessity. Even as Britain was declining, especially in comparison to the United States, there were strong reasons for maintaining the special relationship.

During the more immediate postwar period, the record, as already outlined, has been ambiguous. On the one hand, the Cold War brought the two nations more closely together. On the other, greater dependence on the US, associated with international decline, inevitably changed the relationship from its previous tone. There was resentment of the need to be underwritten by American power, with the attendant condition of being subject to American dictates. Related to this, the shrinking British economic, military—and hence political—position over time encouraged a growing focus on Europe, making ties to other nations of less consequence. The fact that Britain was becoming a regional power, while the Americans were still able to think and act in global terms, created both vertical and horizontal distance between the nations. British foreign policy was less important to the US because of differences in outlook and perspective, and related contrasts in geographical areas of concern.

The difference in the British role in the effort to limit the strategic arms race illustrates this point especially well. Through the 1950s, diplomatic contacts on the subject involved not two superpowers alone, but three great powers—the Soviets, the Americans and the British. During the negotiations over a five-year period to prohibit nuclear tests in the atmosphere, which resulted in the nuclear test-ban treaty of 1963, the British were involved, and in particular Prime Minister Macmillan was active and visible in close discussions with the American President. However, during the Strategic Arms Limitation Talks which gathered momentum from 1968, and especially during the intensive discussions which led to the 1972 SALT I agreement, the British did not play any role at all. In order to reach an accord between the two superpowers, the contacts were limited to those two countries; Europe was consciously and specifically excluded, and Britain was clearly regarded as a European nation. While Britain has never qualified as a superpower in the way in which the term has been employed since the Second World War, in earlier postwar years there was at least British participation as a nuclear power in arms negotiations between the US and the Soviet Union; by the early 1970s, this was no longer the case, for the British arsenal was entirely dwarfed by the enormous nuclear capacities of the other two nations, and Britain was a distinctly secondary international political actor. [20]

The change in the special relationship has been significant in this sense of the implications of British decline, and also for the manner in which British policy has addressed a shifting situation. Consideration of Anglo-American relations reinforces points already made about the character of British foreign policy, both historically and recently. The relationship with the Americans has changed in the sense of being more unequal, as the difference in power between the two countries has grown; it has remained constant in terms of British commitment to a close collaborative arrangement. Moreover, this changing situation and altered balance between the two allies has not been accompanied by an explicit, conscious re-evaluation of the special tie. Instead, there has been gradual adjustment to an altered set of circumstances. The special relationship has been maintained in terms of British interest in harmonious transatlantic affairs. It has survived both entry into Europe and general international decline in part because the British have not drawn attention to the fact that circumstances have been shifting.

Suez, it might be argued, indicates a different situation, where the British were willing to sacrifice the relationship for the sake of recouping face in the Middle East. However, that disaster is more appropriately seen as being out of tune with the general British approach to policy and policy-making. To be sure, it was because great power status was surrendered only reluctantly that a few key officials were willing to undertake the Suez invasion. In these terms, the adventure was certainly congruent with traditional great-power diplomacy. More important, nevertheless, is the point that Suez also represents a marked departure from the way foreign policy is generally undertaken in the British government. There was no broad consultation within the government, or even within the professional foreign policy bureaucracy. Rather, Eden and a few trusted associates decided on the course very much in isolation from the rest of the government, then forced the action on their colleagues. The civil service was kept in the dark; the Cabinet was informed, by all reports, only to approve, not to evaluate. While Suez was reminiscent of past great power, if only by showing the degree to which the nation had declined from that status, it was more starkly out of conformity with standard policy procedures.

Further, the new government under Macmillan, succeeding Eden's, moved immediately to repair the serious damage which had been done to relations with the United States. With considerable success, the new Prime Minister, in a comparatively short period of time, was able to re-establish the confidence and regular consultation which had been a principal feature of Anglo-American relations since the war. Ultimately, the reaction to Suez reinforced the importance of the special relationship to Britain.

If consideration of the special relationship reinforces the observations already made about the characteristics of British foreign policy, it also draws attention to the significance of organisational structure in making and implementing policy. If personality at the highest levels has been important to Anglo-American understanding, so has broader interchange and bureaucratic relationships between the two governments at lower levels. The special relationship has existed in terms of good personal relations between a series of men leading each government; it has also been present, however, in the much more diverse, less visible interchange between the two foreign policy bureaucracies. This interconnection has not prevented Suez and Skybolt crises; it has made them the exception rather the rule, discordant notes in a generally harmonious and understood set of relationships between the two sides. These professional relationships have, in fact, helped to minimise the effects of particular crises such as these at the highest levels.

Just as the ties among various government departments and the Brussels bureaucracy have been used to encourage and make real British involvement in the European Economic Community, so the Anglo-American bureaucratic interchange has been a factor in the continuing success of this relationship. At the centre of the process is the British embassy in Washington; Britain, as the lesser partner, has to make more of an effort to reach the American ear. The embassy is, by design, an exceptionally large headquarters of diplomacy. It is extremely well staffed, with an enormous number of conventional diplomatic, financial and seconded domestic civil servants in residence. It is very much the locus of British diplomacy toward the US, in contrast to the American embassy in London. The embassy staff engages not only in formal meetings and consultations with American counterparts, but also in continuing informal communication and interchange. As one foreign policy analyst has observed concerning this state of affairs:

In London and Washington—and indeed in many other capitals where British and American officials find themselves working together—this often finds expression in committee meetings at a departmental level which provide for regular consultation and discussion over a wide range of matters of common concern.

The working relationships . . . not only guarantee a smooth discharge of decisions arrived at at the highest levels, they reflect and create a climate of common purpose and frank discussion. Consequently, they persist, by a healthy momentum of their own, even when, as at Suez, rupture and conflict impair the functioning of "the highest levels".[21]

In total, therefore, the special relationship has both changed and remained constant over time, depending upon the aspects stressed. Continuously, over virtually the entire history of the United States, there has been the perception on both sides that war is best avoided and other European powers should be restrained from intervention in the affairs of the North American continent. Even when events, late in the last century, seemed to be drawing the two towards war, the ultimate clash was avoided, and seemed bizarre in retrospect simply because the informal accord was so close and reliable. The close collaboration of the twentieth century, as a result, may have been compelled by events, but also rested on a very substantial historical base. More recently, there has been continuity to British policy in terms of the great importance given to understanding with the United States; maintaining accord with the new superpower was given a conscious immediacy it did not have when Britain was the global power. Again, the British have been quite loyal to this policy over time.

Changes have also occurred, but they have taken place within the general context of this consistent and stable framework of Anglo-American relations. It is in specific terms that there have been alterations; in broad terms the special relationship has been distinctive because it has not changed very much, and has drawn strength and continuity from the very general character of the mutual understanding. The resiliency of the accord has been reflected in the fact that the balance of power between the two partners has changed so dramatically, with the United States emerging as an ascendant global power as Britain has declined to an economically hard-pressed regional power, while the comparatively abstract links between them have held firm. As Britain has diminished in power it has been increasingly important to hold the American ear; more subtly, as the United States has struggled with the frustrations, crises and compromises which accompany very great power, it has not been uncongenial to have the reliability of the British alliance. As Atlantic relations have become more uncertain in recent years, with the Americans pursuing condominium and bilateral negotiations with other actual and emerging superpowers removed from Europe, the NATO Alliance in disrepair, and economic difficulties and conflicts growing, the special relationship may not have gained visibility, but it has certainly not lost usefulness or appeal from the American point of view.

6 The Necessity for Accommodation

Has British foreign policy since the second World War been a success or failure? The answer to such a stark question is not easily given, at least if there is interest in an accurate reflection of the complexity of policy and decision-making. Rather, the more reasonable approach is to evaluate the degree to which national policy has pursued realistic ends, the means employed have been appropriate, and desired goals have been realised. In this concluding section of the study, an effort will be made to address this general subject, again from the specific viewpoint of Atlantic Area international relations. Earlier chapters have provided an opportunity to review, analyse and reflect upon the nation's foreign relations from several policy perspectives. The present one attempts to draw together and build upon evidence already presented.

Different analysts have given conflicting answers to the question of the skill and effectiveness with which British foreign policy has been conducted. As noted in the first chapter, a number of American and British observers have in recent years concluded that, on balance, the record is negative. Such a development is hardly surprising, given the general British decline in power and influence during the decades since the Second World War. Earlier praise of the political system was related to great eminence in international politics. The stability and liberty associated with the domestic political system, therefore, was not the only element in the calculus; there was also impressiveness and success in the foreign policy field. More recently, as the nation has grown weaker, power has waned, and both domestic and foreign political problems have grown more severe, those who evaluate foreign policy and domestic politics have become more sceptical and critical, again reflecting a correlation between international developments and attitudes toward the domestic political system.

Whether or not political institutions and practices within Britain are admired, criticism has been focused on the character of the nation's foreign policy. The complaint has been common that the British have lacked decisiveness in choice among policies or clarity in objectives. It is not just that decline has occurred, but the quality of the retreat which causes a negative reaction. Criticism has been voiced precisely because British policy has been at least to some extent reactive. The argument runs that decline could have been minimised, certainly prevented in the extreme degree which developed, had British leadership acted more skilfully—meaning more decisively and quickly—to draw in and concentrate resources by cutting back broad international involvements. Kenneth Waltz has made a particularly pertinent and biting assessment on this point, yet represents a fairly general attitude among American observers of British foreign policy. He writes: "From the mid-1950s onward, a more forthright explication of Britain's situation and the limited choices open to her, and fewer words about Commonwealth, special relations, unique contributions, and how good one was having it, would have served the country better."[1]

Commonly, this point is linked to the extensive conception of "three circles". Had at least one, and preferably two, been surrendered, so the thesis runs, there would have been an opportunity for greater effect on the area which remained. More concretely, British sluggishness in accepting the fact that the future of the nation's foreign policy rested with Europe, while clinging to a Commonwealth which was too broad and extensive, and a superpower partner which was too strong, are cited as primary instances of this lack of foresight. The possibility of having great influence in a particular sector has been overridden by the desire to maintain connections in all three. Henry Kissinger has been quoted along this line at the beginning of the study, and the observation is hardly unique to him. As Stanley Hoffmann observed in writing about the character of Atlantic Area international relations, comparing Britain in a critical way to the other nations of the region: "A policy of keeping all options open has narrowed them all and narrowed Britain's role. Britain's new approach to the Common Market shows little willingness to resolve these ambiguities."[2]

The criticism of scholars has been in tune with that of decision-makers on this point. This is true despite the strength of anglophilia in foreign policy circles during the years right after the war. Dean Acheson's remark about the British having lost an empire without finding a satisfactory alternative role was one way of referring to this alleged indecisiveness. While he got special attention for this statement, the fact remains that the declaration was not unique or singular to him. The existence of a special relationship with the British did not detract from the fact that the borders of the partner's foreign policy appeared to many observers to be indistinctly defined.

British attitudes toward their own nation's foreign policy have been more mixed if considered in the broadest terms, with some sympathetic and positive evaluations in conventional scholarly circles. To repeat a point made at the start, following the Second World War, and especially since the enormous trauma of Suez, a large amount of literature has been produced which is strongly and broadly self-critical in nature. Often, foreign policy matters are dealt with only indirectly, in the context of very general cultural criticism. Reflecting postwar decline, British critics—like many American observers—have difficulty in maintaining any sense of complacency about the efficacy of political institutions, cultural traditions and social practices. The Angry Young Man set of literary cynics in the mid-1950s were representative of a much broader sense of insecurity about the changing national role and position.

On the other hand, generally in more scholarly circles, there has been some praise for the manner in which foreign policy has been conducted, with a tendency at times to emphasise the importance of residual influence and argue the case that policy has reacted sensibly to the changing international status of the nation. Understandably, this literature looks more to foreign policy directly than to the domestic factors. External restraints receive more attention than internal shortcomings. F. S. Northedge is quite representative of this positive approach in assessing foreign affairs developments since the Second World War:

> The proper understanding of foreign policy demands compassion. But it also requires the appreciation of conditions and forces at work outside the Cabinet room which are often by no means what the responsible authorities would wish. Especially is this true for a country which, like Britain, has had to accommodate itself within a brief span of sixteen years to the momentous changes described in this book.

David Vital goes much further in his very favourable evaluation of the British position: "Viewed summarily and without regard for past splendours modern Britain cannot but be reckoned a very considerable and well-endowed member of the contemporary international community."[3]

It is not surprising that some American and British observers have had conflicting interpretations of basic outlines of the latter nation's foreign policy. Over the past three decades, British policy has remained generally continuous with established attitudes and approaches. The national situation has changed drastically; the outlook on specific foreign policies, decision-making, and relations with the wider world generally has not altered much if at all. It is the world, the international system, and the economic resources available to Britain which have been transformed, not the basic foreign policy style itself. Consequently, there are British analysts, familiar and comfortable with their own culture, who have seen comparatively little to criticise in the way policy has been handled.

Americans concerned with British foreign policy, on the other hand, are part of a very different political culture, and developments since the Second World War have accentuated such differences. From 1945 onward, there has been, in contrast to the past, a broad yet intimate American involvement in international relations, with corresponding abandonment of traditional isolationism. British institutions and practices were admired not only during a period when that country was a very great power, but also when the US was quite literally a distant, removed observer of important developments in the world. Once the Americans were themselves involved in a range of foreign commitments and entanglements, it was more difficult to regard the British with such admiration. Close alliance would probably inevitably have led to some frictions; moreover, the British taste for ambiguity, subtle movements and accommodation grated on the very different American style.

This point should be stressed. The general similarity between domestic political institutions of the two countries, and the enormous and myriad British influence on the US, can easily conceal differences that are significant to foreign policy. History has conspired with cultural predispositions to give British and American foreign policy very different orientations. The British, following upon a long history of involvement in complex and changing European relations, have emphasised flexibility and willingness to compromise. By contrast, the US was confronted soon after the Second World War with an international system already frozen into two rigidly opposed *blocs*. As the unchallenged leader of one side in the confrontation, it would have been difficult for the Americans to employ a British approach even had they wished to do so.

From the British side, the very same characteristics of postwar international affairs, while representing a drastic change from the traditional European system, did not encourage departures in approach. Quite the contrary, from the British point of view rather than the American, the directness of the confrontation between the two superpowers encouraged efforts to pursue a mediating role. Hence, developments since the war have magnified and enlarged fundamental contrasts between British and American ideas about foreign policy.

While American attitudes may strongly encourage criticism of British policy, especially in the light of the postwar experiences of both countries, there remains the separate issue of the appropriateness of the British policy response to the new and changing international environment. In reviewing the manner in which the British have handled the decline from international eminence, loss of empire, contraction of military power, and general redirection of foreign policy toward Europe, there are a number of positive observations which can be made.

First, and most generally, beyond the criticism which has been levelled at the British approach, there is the fact that the nation's leaders have been able to accomplish an enormous shift in international position, power and responsibilities without experiencing drastic instabilities or discontinuities in policy. One reason why policy has not been praised is that it has been unaccompanied by special or remarkable drama. The steadiness and general predictability of British retreat in the face of a changing environment and a shrinking economic base lacked flair or excitement. Because policy has been unexciting, there has been a tendency to minimise successful aspects. The smoothness and stability with which the British shift has been accomplished has made the transition appear comparatively easy to manage. The character of success has been bland and unspecific; possibilities for failure have been underestimated because of the same basic stability. Another country might have stumbled badly in the course of adjusting to so many large changes; other European countries did suffer costly wars and diplomatic reversals in the course of withdrawal from much less substantial colonial empires. The British were successful in facilitating as well as accepting great change with a minimum of strain and instability.

From the second, related perspective of domestic politics, it is clear that the British have been able to achieve this substantial international reorientation with minimal disruptions at home. Again, the ease with which the shift has been accomplished understates the fact that it has been very far-reaching and might have been expected to generate considerably more domestic debate and controversy than in fact took place. Other nations of Europe, with less extensive colonial empires, military capacities and international influence, have nevertheless reacted to the decolonisation experience, and accompanying military and diplomatic problems, with considerably more domestic instability than the British. It is often pointed out that the French moved more quickly and clearly than the British in cutting loose from lingering colonial ties in order to concentrate their efforts on Europe and the Atlantic. It should be noted more frequently that the British generally avoided military swamps comparable to Algeria and Indochina, handled the wars in which they did become engaged—such as the conflicts in Aden and Malaysia—with more dispatch and effectiveness, and maintained broad involvements in part because of comparatively friendly relations with former colonial areas.

This success reflected the fact that the stability and orderliness of domestic politics permitted great latitude and initiative to foreign policy decision-makers. The more rigid and divided character of French politics encouraged both persistence in military engagements after they had become disasters, and quick changes in policy to re-establish domestic support. In Britain, the political left has been consistently active and critical of foreign policy, but only occasionally able to muster really substantial support within the Labour Party. The far right has had in recent years some very articulate spokesmen, including Enoch Powell, but has been unable to develop an effective challenge to the generally moderate Conservative Party leadership. The lack of foreign and domestic instabilities resulting from international readjustment are, therefore, important joint testimony to the strength of British political culture and institutions.

Along with accepting international decline, and doing so with minimal domestic disruption, the British have clearly over time concentrated increasing foreign policy resources and attention upon Europe. This shows not only that the reality of a much-reduced international position has been accepted; it also indicates that the principal region of interest and connection, for the present and likely future, appropriately has been recognised to be Europe. Britain has become one of several middle-ranking European powers rather than a great international power which stands entirely or nearly alone. Military resources are no longer sufficient to maintain large outposts and patrol the seas around the world. They are, however, still capable of making a very useful contribution to NATO defence. The Commonwealth is comparatively much less important to the British economy, West Europe much more. These facts have been accepted fairly gradually, but they have been accepted. The change has been reflected in the emphasis given to the European Economic Community by successive British governments, in the very explicit focus on European defence in the latest military forces review, and most fundamentally and broadly in the results of the popular referendum on the Common Market.

Appreciation for the movement toward greater emphasis on Europe is a useful antidote to allegations that the British have been unwilling to yield to the demands of political reality. They have instead been responsive, but in characteristic fashion. The need to give primacy to Europe over the Commonwealth has been accepted, but once again this has been done gradually rather than abruptly. In earlier years, foreign policy might have appeared to be favouring one commitment above the others. Moreover, the rhetoric of political leaders, especially in extolling the virtues of the special relationship with the United States and the different—but also very strong—emotional ties to the Commonwealth, often seemed to be searching everywhere but Europe for clues to the best future directions of national policy. In reality, from the present period looking backward, the British have been moving for a number of years toward closer involvement with Europe. Rhetoric is one thing, the specifics of policy and concrete commitments another. The special relationship is praised, but virtually no one in British government and politics believes the nation is on anything approaching equality with the two superpowers. The Commonwealth contains myriad strong and gripping memories, but is hardly a focus for foreign policy currently. It was not Europe which was rejected at Messina, only a certain structural mechanism which was out of tune with the traditional conception of European relations. This was reversed in 1961; it was de Gaulle who prevented entry for a number of years after that, not the thrust of British foreign policy.

Related to criticism about failure to change quickly enough to meet new international conditions is the point that the British lacked good foresight concerning the shifting position and role of the nation, especially in the years just after the Second World War. Long before that war, for example, there was hard evidence that Britain's economic position in the world, on which great political power in turn had been based, was declining. Right after the war, it was certainly clear in economic terms that Britain lacked the resources to keep up with the two emerging superpowers.

Yet, given the force of Britain's historical position, it is not surprising that few observers concentrated on this. Epstein's remark about the difficulty of seeing the British as anything but the "top dogs" internationally returns to mind. Indeed, the British were not alone in the belief that they would be able to maintain eminence. The American international affairs specialist William T. R. Fox, writing in the closing days of the Second World War, was representative of attitudes in his country about probable British influence after the end of hostilities: "There is no mystery about which will be the powers of first rank in the postwar world. The United States of America, Great Britain, and the Soviet Union are the Big Three in war as they will be in peace."[4] Foresight is always a rare commodity, in foreign policy as in other fields; the fact that the British have not always possessed the quality is worthy of note really only because the changes which have developed since the war have been so drastic.

Moreover, while the British might have acted more decisively and quickly in the effort to adapt to the new international situation, that course carried significant risks. It is possible that the embarrassment of rejection might have been avoided had the decision to enter the Common Market been made sooner; certainly this would have been the case had the British joined when they had the opportunity at the establishment of the new institutions in the late 1950s. At the same time, there is the point that more rapid and decisive action might also easily have led to greater international disruptions, blunders and instability, and more bitterness and controversy within the domestic political system. It is common to criticise British foreign policy for lack of imagination and innovation. The reverse point about potential costs to this alternative course is not made frequently enough.

Attitudes which have led to this negative perception of British policy are not difficult to understand. It remains uncertain what might have taken place if particular problems and issues had been handled differently; there is at least the possibility that more excitement and novelty in foreign relations would have created, on balance, more success as well as more interest. But if policy can be made to suffer through comparison with hypothetical alternative courses, it is important to underline the reservation that more adventurousness could also have led to great reversals. Whether different policies would have produced better results is simply not known.

An entirely persuasive case cannot be made by developing this line of argument, thanks to the fact that it involves supposition and speculation about what might have occurred had other policy avenues been pursued. At the same time, it is reasonable to assume that had there not been an emphasis on good continuing working relationships with the United States, more crises along the lines of Suez and Skybolt would very probably have taken place. Indeed, the very fact that Britain was heavily in debt to the Americans for economic assistance made close sensitivity to the ally's views virtually inevitable. Similarly, had the British Commonwealth ties been abruptly servered, the reverberations would have been quite severe in both British politics and the economies of many Commonwealth countries.

One way to conceptualise British foreign policy developments since the Second World War is to think in terms of the international arena not as three circles, but simply as one very large parameter, which has gradually grown smaller thanks primarily to the declining British economic capacity. Economic weakness at home has changed the nature of the special relationship with the Americans, forced the British to surrender global military commitments, and generally reduced freedom and initiative in foreign affairs. At the same time, the economic incentive of close longstanding ties, and more recent indebtedness, has encouraged maintaining contact with the Americans, while developing trade patterns have moved the country closer to Europe. Economic strictures gradually have grown tighter; foreign policy gradually has been adjusted, with a constantly more apparent narrowing and focusing on the locus of Continental ties.

The British style may be contrasted with that of other major nations in the Atlantic Area. Less restricted economically, often possessing a more dramatic flair than the British, it remains debatable whether or not their foreign policies have really been superior. Both West Germany and, especially, France have made strenuous efforts to operate distinctive foreign policies in order to reach independent accords with the Soviet Union. In the case of the *Ostpolitik*, under Chancellor Brandt of West Germany, especially during the years 1969–73, substantial new agreements were reached with the Soviets and other Warsaw Pact nations concerning the legitimacy of borders, status of Berlin, and other matters. Clearly this was a victory for West German foreign policy, providing testimony to the skill of the Chancellor and his associates. For our purposes, however, it is important to bear in mind as well the unique geographical and historical position of West Germany, which provided an opportunity for these settlements. After the treaties were signed, the psychological and political momentum behind *Ostpolitik* began to dissipate, underlining the importance of the postwar territorial situation in providing the incentive for accommodation.

France under de Gaulle pursued an even more strongly independent foreign policy. It involved not just initiatives undertaken separately from the Americans, but outright hostility to American leadership of the Atlantic Alliance, resulting in direct symbolic and political challenges to successive American Administrations (and in particular to the Kennedy Administration), frustration of British hopes to enter the Common Market, and greater division generally within the Alliance. Though this policy lent considerable interest and excitement to Atlantic relations, however, it is difficult to see where and how de Gaulle was able to have a permanent, or even long-term, impact on the Alliance or more limited European affairs. He kept the British out of the EEC, but they got in soon after he left office. He stressed the lesson to his Common Market partners that the nation-state is not easily subordinated to supranational institutions, but others—including the British in particular—were willing and able to make the same point. Indeed, his point about the resilience of the national unit depended for validity on the fact that none of the Community partners were anxious to surrender important amounts of sovereignty to the supranational goal. French withdrawal from NATO, with the inconvenience of forcing the headquarters to move from Paris, hardly changed the reality of American military dominance or the fact that a general war in Europe is most unlikely to take place without French participation on the Allied side. Recent French steps to move back towards NATO in terms of practical military co-ordination underline this point.

Finally, there have been great contrasts between British and American approaches to foreign policy, already discussed in terms of both cultural attitudes and structural features. The Americans do have clear advantages in terms of the openness of foreign policy decision-making to significant, at times creative, departures from the *status quo*. There is more variability among the individuals in power over time, hence greater opportunity to bring fresh ideas to bear. For this very reason, however, there is a tendency for American observers to underestimate the contrasting British strengths. American foreign policy, in the Atlantic area as elsewhere, has at times highlighted the sorts of problems resulting from lack of co-ordination and absence of continuity. There is the example of the great European uncertainty generated by the abrupt American switch in defence policy from Eisenhower-style massive retaliation to Kennedy-style flexible response. During the Johnson Administration, the dependence of important foreign policy decisions on a few personalities, and the distraction of those men by the Vietnam War in the middle and late 1960s, led in consequence to an ignoring of European problems and a drift in European policy. This was followed not by a consistent

American effort to restore good diplomatic relations in the Atlantic Area, but rather by a confused mixture of signals, in which declarations about the need for friendship were followed by efforts to create frictions to facilitate broader policy goals, only to be succeeded by the declaration that 1973 was to be the "Year of Europe".

Again, the continuity of British foreign policy toward the United States over time reflects more than the felt need to maintain the special relationship. American shifts in policy, and the frequent confusion attending them, contrast with British appreciation for the advantages of general consistency. For the British, the ongoing need to maintain good relations with the Americans has merged easily with a broader tradition of the importance of continuity in policy.

POLICY STRUCTURE AND STYLE

Along with the overall stability with which great transformations abroad have been accepted at home, there is the related consideration that aspects of Britain's decision-making structures and foreign policy style have worked to foster gradualism and consistency. As·described earlier, foreign policy is made by politicians and civil servants who have been involved with the established system, existing procedures and conventional attitudes for a number of years before they reach the top. The political and administrative socialisation process reinforces the professional emphasis within the government on broad consultation among different interested departments before decisions are made. With the powerful pressures for consensus which this system encourages, there is little likelihood that there will be many serious abrupt changes in policy.

In this sense, cultural predispositions and the traditional conservatism of foreign policy have been reinforced by structural characteristics. Indeed, it might be argued that in recent decades these consensual and conservative qualities of public policy in Britain have grown more pronounced. Samuel Beer, among other observers, has argued that the direct access of interest groups to the centres of policy decision has increased in force and effectiveness. As public policy has become more far-reaching in society, as well as increasingly complex, there has been an incentive for organised national producer and consumer groups to try to shape policy, and for decision-makers to seek out their specialised information and expertise. The interchange between government officials and interest representatives has therefore become more close and intense. At the same time, the growth in party discipline in Parliament, while not removing that arena as a centre for public debate and discussion, has made governments more secure and independent, with increased policy initiative.

Impressed by the strength of such groups, in tandem with modern party discipline, Beer concluded that a situation has emerged in which any major departure in policy would likely be vetoed by one or more influential national interests.[5] Generalising from this point, one can argue that contemporary functional representation, in the field of foreign affairs, will tend strongly to reinforce the established tradition of slow-moving and conservative change. As a corollary, the acquiescence of such groups would appear more important than ever in decisions which affect their concerns. A principal piece of evidence for this general proposition is offered by Robert Lieber's examination of Britain's relationship with the Common Market, where changes in government policy correlated directly with shifts in attitude among concerned interest groups.

INCREMENTALISM AND FOREIGN POLICY

In reflecting on the character, past and present, of British foreign policy, a principal conclusion is that the style of decision-making and policy development has been representative of what Charles Lindblom has termed the incremental approach. Lindblom's classic path-breaking analysis of the policy process defined two basic approaches to making decisions: incrementalism and rational policy-making.[6] As the word implies, incrementalism refers to changes which are small-scale. Rather than resulting in sweeping or comprehensive alterations in the *status quo*, this style creates generally marginal shifts and slight transitions. Normally, such decisions are made on the basis of partial and imperfect information, rather than a comprehensive review, which in turn encourages limitation in scope. From another perspective, incrementalism is a sensitive process, because decision-makers, who are involved in a sequence of choices, and therefore close to the evolving policy situation, are able to adjust and re-evaluate on the basis of unfolding results. In contrast to incrementalism, Lindblom places rational decision-making, in which change tends to be very large and imposed, after quite thorough study of likely consequences. This effort to predict policy outcomes accurately involves the employment of sophisticated cost–benefit statistical analysis.

In the real world, the argument continues, most decisions are incremental rather than comprehensive. These kinds of decisions are ". . . the decisions typical of ordinary political life—even if they rarely solve problems but merely stave them off or nibble at them, often making headway but sometimes retrogressing. Decisions like these are made day by day in ordinary political circumstances by congressmen, executives, administrators and party leaders." Lindblom's point is not only that incremental decisions are desirable because this process is sensitive to complex reality and adjustable, but also that this approach is actually the one used by most decision-makers. In a democracy like the United States, with complicated established institutional structures and processes for developing and implementing public policy, there are powerful pressures for incrementalism. Acceptable change must be capable of satisfying the diverse array of influential interest groups, and therefore tends to be rather cautious. More adventurous departure from established patterns runs the risk of antagonising enough groups to be vetoed or result in defeat at the polls. In a similar manner, democratic politicians, sensitive to the general thrust of public opinion, generally compete strenuously only at the margins of existing policy. The basic characteristics of public policy are accepted by political parties and politicians in the effort to increase popular support.[7]

From the viewpoint of the concerns in this study, Britain could be described as an even better example than the United States of a system which encourages, indeed generally requires, that an incremental approach be used. To be sure, there are at times comprehensive policy evaluations, with the possibility of sweeping reform as a result. Government White Papers are an especially important device for reflecting upon the course of policy in a particular area. In actual practice, however, as we have seen, British foreign policy is characterised very strongly by small rather than large changes. The British emphasis on co-ordination and consultation throughout the government ensures that incremental influences will be pronounced. Possible risks and costs of policy alternatives are considered at length, and the interests of diverse departments and their constituents are taken carefully into account before any decision of consequence is made. Interest groups are fully and effectively represented in the corridors of administrative power.

Viewed broadly, this has resulted in a British foreign policy which has been conservative but not entirely rigid or frozen. A point which recurs repeatedly when considering British policy in the Atlantic Area, and more generally, is that there has been accommodation to new realities and changed circumstances, albeit of a generally slow and gradual kind. The consideration of postwar policies toward the Common Market and European co-operation generally, the United States and national defence leads uniformly toward the conclusion that the dominant quality of foreign relations has been continuity. The shifts which have occurred have almost never been rapid or sweeping, and the British have moved to accept change normally in piecemeal fashion. Even the 1961 turnaround on policy toward the European Economic Community was the small public tip of a large private iceberg that involved very complex and extensive interchange among different sectors of the bureaucracy, with interested departments changing position at varying rates before the government as a whole turned and the Prime Minister announced that application for membership would be made.

Britain's Common Market policy also may be used to illustrate the structural flexibility within the government bureaucracy. Over time, the locus of decision-making and co-ordination has changed from the Board of Trade, to the Foreign Office, to the Cabinet Office, with closely related responsibilities often clearly divided between different departments—for example, in making one responsible for general co-ordination, and others for providing specific expertise to aid the negotiations themselves. These shifts, changes and alterations in the linkages of policy responsibility have generally been handled smoothly, without great disruptions accompanying reshuffling of authority.

Examining structural relationships in the somewhat different context of their capacity to be changed leads to the point that clearly British emphasis on incrementalism has not prevented carrying through effective administrative reforms when they have been regarded as necessary. The transformation of defence organisation, undertaken over a period of several years but nevertheless quite sweeping, is evidence for the point that, in foreign policy as in domestic, the British are capable not only of deciding to change things drastically, but also of implementing such reforms. British success in centralising planning and co-ordination of defence policy stands in contrast to the strenuous effort to do the same in the United States in the 1960s, the results of which were at best uncertain, and ultimately voided when a new Republican Administration took power at the end of the decade.

The process of consultation and co-ordination on policy is therefore double-edged in result. It works to make policy conservative, with especially powerful incentives to hold to the *status quo*. At the same time, once decisions have been made, even if they are sweeping in nature, implementation can be handled swiftly and effectively. The unusually close and efficient co-ordination among civil servants ensures that the distance between decision and implementation, between choices by leaders and movement by the bureaucracy, is small. It also makes structural reforms generally easy to carry out. American practices, by contrast, help make policy novel and innovative at times, but ensure continuing and often self-defeating competition among different sectors of the government, with a strong possibility that the *status quo* will survive and reform efforts will be defeated by the existing mutual veto system, and that policy, when implemented, may represent a very jarring shift with unforeseen consequences.

Evaluations of the British foreign policy process should not be cast in terms which are too onesidedly complimentary. General co-ordination works well within the bureaucracy because of the effectiveness of flexible interdepartmental committees, at both formal and informal levels, and the more diffuse network of personal understanding and communication. At the same time, in Britain as in the US, there has been growing interest in improving intragovernmental communication through weakening the barriers which stand between the foreign and domestic policy sectors. As described earlier, there are important, if generally abstract and psychological, divisions between these two sides of the civil service profession. Contemporary international relations, however, involve economic and other sorts of technical issues which have a comparatively strong bearing on policy, especially in comparison with the earlier postwar period. This means that multilateral diplomacy often involves the domestic departments of a government as much as, and perhaps more than, the Foreign Office. This in turn has led to growing interest in programmes to increase understanding and interchange between domestic and foreign policy environments, usually through seconding professional staff members on short-term bases from one milieu to the other. This has been attempted in Britain, and as elsewhere there has been only modest and limited success. Table 6.1 provides some information on the sort of seconding which has occurred. It shows that numbers involved have been very small, even between the Foreign and Commonwealth Office and the Department of Trade and Industry, which would be presumed to be a priority linkage in a period of severe

TABLE 6.1:   *Seconding of Officers between Diplomatic
and Domestic Services*

Domestic departments	From the diplomatic service	To the diplomatic service
Trade/Industry	26	36
Defence	1	26
Home Office	0	28
Cabinet Office	17	2
Overseas Development	2	15
Employment	1	12
Environment	1	5
Treasury	0	5
Civil Service	4	1
Energy	2	1
Health/Social Security	1	1
Others	6	20
Totals	61	152

(Source: Foreign and Commonwealth Office. Figures as of 30 September 1975)

international economic problems combined with recent British entry into the Common Market. Clearly, even in the rather fluid British civil service environment, going beyond the interdepartmental committee system to establish stronger formal co-ordination is more easily envisioned than accomplished.

Despite this important reservation, however, the more general observation remains valid that the British model of achieving co-ordination in foreign policy remains impressive and perhaps instructive. Since the Second World War, the British have adjusted, retreated and changed internationally in order to accommodate drastically altered conditions, and more slow-moving economic developments which could no longer be ignored. High drama and momentous conflict have largely been absent. Rather, the British lesson has been one of a nation trying to minimise losses and reversals, protect residual influence and promote stability in a manner very much in tune with the traditional approach to foreign affairs. In this, they have been aided by a political culture, established institutions, and policy style which have emphasised stability and gradualism, accommodation and co-ordination. The British achievement has not been to reverse decline or expand influence and power, but to move with change, to focus increasingly on the Atlantic Area and Europe, to make adjustment look easy to handle smoothly. No longer a great power in the world, the British finally are possibly in an especially good position to illustrate the importance of co-ordination between domestic and foreign policy departments in the conduct of international affairs. In this sense, the Common Market, far from being a final stopping-point on the road of retreat, provides an opportunity to address complex and technical problems of policy development of a sort for which the British may be particularly well suited.

Notes and References

Chapter 1

1. For a useful discussion of the development of the Anglo-American alliance, which argues that it has strong historical roots, see Coral Bell, *The Debatable Alliance* (London: Oxford University Press, 1964), passim and especially pp. 1–23.
2. Henry Kissinger, *The Troubled Partnership* (New York: Doubleday and Co., 1965), p. 77.
3. Kenneth Waltz, *Foreign Policy and Democratic Politics* (Boston: Little, Brown and Co., 1967), p. 234.
4. See for example F. H. Hinsley, *Power and the Pursuit of Peace* (Cambridge: The University Press, 1963), pp. 256ff. In 1891, the Triple Alliance of Germany, Austria and Italy was extended for twelve years, and the following year France and Russia agreed to continue their military alliance for the duration of the Triple Alliance. Before this, alliances had been made for shorter periods of three to five years. Britain resisted this trend, but found herself sucked in; in the 1887 Mediterranean Agreements, a long-term commitment was undertaken.
5. In Walter Bagehot's *The English Constitution* (London: Collins, 1963) see especially the contrast in chapter 1 between Cabinet and Presidential government. The American habit of praising British politics, often misunderstanding it in the process, is discussed by Evron Kirkpatrick, "Toward a More Responsible Two-Party System: Political Science, or Pseudo-Science?" *American Political Science Review*, Vol. LXV, No. 4 (December 1971), pp. 965–90.
6. Concerning this contrast, see for example Hugh Heclo and Aaron Wildavsky, *The Private Government of Public Money* (Berkeley: University of California Press, 1974), pp. 9–10.
7. *Encounter*, Vol. XXI (July 1963); also see for example Brian Chapman, *British Government Observed* (London: Allen and Co., 1963); John Osborne, *The Entertainer* (New York: Criterion Books, 1958); James Morris, *The Outriders* (London: Faber and Faber, 1963).
8. Hans Morgenthau, *Politics Among Nations* (New York: Alfred Knopf, 1948), p. 189.
9. Waltz, op. cit., pp. 3–6.
10. Ibid., pp. 7–8.
11. See Winston Churchill, *The Gathering Storm* (Boston: Houghton Mifflin, 1948), chapter 4.

12. On the changing structure of the international system, see Stanley Hoffmann, *Gulliver's Troubles* (New York: McGraw-Hill, 1968), p. 10 and chapter 2.

13. Waltz, op. cit., pp. 5–6, on the differences between the British and American great power positions. He emphasises contrasts and minimises or denies similarities.

14. Kissinger, op. cit., pp. 76–7.

15. Leon Epstein, *Britain—Uneasy Ally* (Chicago: University of Chicago Press, 1954), p. 9.

16. F. S. Northedge, *British Foreign Policy—The Process of Readjustment 1945–1961* (London: George Allen and Unwin Ltd., 1962), p. 32.

17. See Waltz, op. cit., pp. 80–1 for pertinent remarks concerning Bevin's views on his experience as Foreign Secretary, and the manner in which the British have managed concensus between the two parties on foreign policy without formal bipartisanship.

18. Northedge, op. cit., pp. 57ff.

19. George Kennan, *Memoirs 1925–1950* (Boston: Little Brown and Co., 1967), pp. 314–22.

20. Epstein, op. cit., p. 10, quoting a London speech on 11 June 1952.

21. Richard Rosecrance, *Defense of the Realm* (New York: Columbia University Press, 1968), p. 45.

22. Epstein, op. cit., pp. 114–15.

23. Charles de Gaulle, *The Complete War Memoirs* (New York: Simon and Schuster, 1968), p. 557.

24. Northedge, op. cit., p. 137.

25. Ibid., p. 44; Rosecrance, op. cit., p. 69.

26. Alfred Havighurst, *Twentieth-Century Britain* (New York: Harper and Row, 1962), pp. 409, 462.

27. Rosecrance, op. cit., pp. 6–7.

28. Richard Neustadt, *Alliance Politics* (New York: Columbia University Press, 1970), pp. 30–55.

29. Waltz, op. cit., p. 306.

30. Havighurst, op. cit., pp. 15–17.

31. Waltz, op. cit., p. 23.

32. Northedge, op. cit., pp. 33–4.

33. Ibid., p. 34.

34. Ibid., pp. 33–7.

35. Epstein, op. cit., p. 39.

36. Phyllis Deana and W. A. Cole, *British Economic Growth 1688–1959* (London: Cambridge University Press, 1962), Table 73.

37. Loc. cit.

38. Richard Caves and associates, *Britain's Economic Prospects* (Washington: The Brookings Institution, 1968), p. 279.

39. Ibid., p. 495.

40. Leon Epstein, "British Foreign Policy", p. 51 in Roy Macridis (ed.), *Foreign Policy in World Politics* (Englewood Cliffs: Prentice-Hall, 1962).

41. Havighurst, op. cit., p. 383.

42. Ibid., p. 399.

43. Samuel Beer, *British Politics in the Collectivist Age* (New York: Alfred Knopf, 1965), 205–7.
44. Havighurst, op. cit., 401–2.
45. Samuel Beer, *The British Political System* (New York: Random House, 1974), pp. 71–2.

Chapter 2

1. Gabriel Almond and Sidney Verba, *The Civic Culture* (Boston: Little, Brown and Co., 1965), p. 35.
2. Waltz, op. cit., p. 36.
3. Richard Neustadt, "White House and Whitehall", *The Public Interest*, II, 1966, pp. 55–69.
4. R. H. S. Crossman, *The Myths of Cabinet Government* (Cambridge: Harvard University Press, 1972) is one of the most prominent recent arguments that the Prime Minister is becoming more presidential (see especially pp. 51–8).
5. Beer, *The British Political System* op. cit., p. 121.
6. See for example, Heclo and Wildavsky, op. cit., chapter 1–3 and passim.
7. Waltz, op. cit., p. 130.
8. Ibid., pp. 130–1.
9. Northedge, op. cit., p. 32 and passim.
10. Donald G. Bishop, *The Administration of British Foreign Relations* (Syracuse University Press, 1961), pp. 74ff.
11. Paul Gore-Booth, *With Great Truth and Respect* (London: Constable, 1974), p. 227.
12. Harold Wilson, *The Labour Government 1964–70–A Personal Record* (Harmondsworth: Penguin Books, 1974), p. 352.
13. Harold Seidman, *Politics, Position and Power—The Dynamics of Federal Organization* (New York: Oxford University Press, 1970), pp. 110–11.
14. Bishop, op. cit., p. 225; D. C. M. Platt, *The Cinderella Service—British Consuls since 1825* (London: Longman, 1971), p. 2.
15. Bishop, pp. 207ff.
16. *Report of the Review Committee on Overseas Representation. 1968–1969*, Sir Val Duncan, Chairman, Cmnd. 4107 (July 1969), p. 21. and passim. See also *Review of Overseas Representation*, Report by the Central Policy Review Staff (HMSO, 1977), especially pp. 305ff.
17. I. M. Destler, *Presidents, Bureaucrats and Foreign Policy—The Politics of Organizational Reform* (Princeton University Press, 1972), p. 25, 30, chapter 5 and passim.
18. Ibid., pp. 96–104.
19. David Vital, *The Making of British Foreign Policy* (London: George Allen and Unwin Ltd., 1968), pp. 59–60.
20. Destler, op. cit., pp. 3, 118ff. on the Nixon–Kissinger system.
21. One of the most useful recent analyses of the Treasury, with particular attention to its international role, is Samuel Brittan, *Steering the Economy* (Harmondsworth: Penguin Books, 1971), passim.
22. Vital, op. cit., p. 52.

23. Destler, op. cit., p. 5.
24. William Bacchus, "Diplomacy for the 70's: An Afterview and Appraisal", *American Political Science Review*, Vol. LXVIII, No. 2 (June 1974), p. 736.
25. Ibid., p. 744.
26. Destler, op. cit., pp. 177–8.
27. Duncan, Cmnd. 4107, op. cit., pp. 25, 29ff.
28. Ibid., pp. 10–13.
29. Brittan, op. cit., pp. 32–3.
30. Duncan, Cmnd. 4107, op. cit., p. 34.
31. Brittan, op. cit., pp. 26–7.

Chapter 3

1. Rosecrance, op. cit., pp. 46–7, 55.
2. Ibid., pp. 84–5.
3. Ibid., p. 121.
4. William P. Snyder, *The Politics of British Defense Policy* (Columbus: Ohio State University Press, 1964), p. 34.
5. Ibid., pp. 34–5.
6. Quoted in Snyder, p. 25.
7. Ibid., pp. 25ff.
8. Ibid., p. 27.
9. Ibid., pp. 28–9.
10. The British are notable for the determination and scientific expertise employed in the development of atomic weapons during the Second World War. British scientific research, at least in the early phases of bomb development, was generally superior to American. To some extent, this reflected the fact that Britain was at war and the US was not; but the Germans and Soviets failed to show equal willpower. See Andrew Pierre, *Nuclear Politics* (London: Oxford University Press, 1972), pp. 20–24.
11. See for example Waltz, op. cit., chapter 7.
12. Rosecrance, op. cit., p. 43.
13. Waltz, op. cit., p. 148.
14. On miscalculations and misperceptions concerning Suez, see Neustadt, *Alliance Politics*, op. cit., especially chapter 2.
15. A number of foreign policy analysts interested in the Atlantic area, including Stanley Hoffmann and Henry Kissinger as well as Rosecrance, have made the point in different contexts that the British were unwilling to choose decisively among various policy alternatives.
16. Snyder, op. cit., pp. 35–6.
17. Ibid., pp. 37–8.
18. Neustadt, *Alliance Politics*, op. cit., especially chapter 3.
19. Wilson, op. cit., pp. 70ff.
20. Ibid., p. 73.
21. Ibid., pp. 112ff.
22. Waltz, op. cit., p. 177.

23. Rosecrance, op. cit., p. 270.
24. Richard Burt, *Defence Budgeting: The British and American Cases* (London: International Institute for Strategic Studies, Adelphi Paper 112, 1975), p. 33.
25. Ibid., passim., places considerable emphasis on the continuity of defence policy over time. On the most recent spending cuts, see for example, *The Economist* (5 March 1977), p. 24.
26. Samuel P. Huntington, *The Common Defense* (New York: Columbia University Press, 1962), p. 118.
27. On McNamara's reforms in the Pentagon and related subjects, see William Kaufmann, *The McNamara Strategy* (New York: Harper and Row, 1964), passim.
28. Huntington, op. cit., p. 135.
29. An interesting discussion of McNamara's conflicts with military and Congressional opponents over Vietnam policy is provided in Townsend Hoopes, *The Limits of Intervention* (New York: David McKay Co. Inc., 1973), pp. 83–91 and passim.
30. The innovation of the Nixon Administration was most likely spurred by a combination of management and political motives. The McNamara system in the Pentagon had developed problems and shortcomings over time, but there was also doubtless a desire to try to gain partisan advantage from removal of one of the most prominent and controversial policies of the Democratic regimes of the 1960s.
31. Burt, op. cit., p. 5.
32. Loc. cit.
33. Heclo and Wildavsky, op. cit., chapter 5 and passim.
34. Burt, op. cit., pp. 4–5.
35. Beer (1965), op. cit., pp. 225–7.
36. See Huntington, op. cit., chapter 6 and passim. on the defence policy debate in the US in the 1950s. He states on p. 218, with considerable foresight:

> No Administration was ever confronted with a united military establishment backing a single coherent military plan. If an Administration had ever been so confronted, it would have been extremely difficult and perhaps impossible for the Administration not to have acquiesced in the military demands. Divided against themselves, however, the military limited themselves. Interservice rivalry was a key element in the control of the Administration over the size of the defence effort.

Chapter 4

1. Nora Beloff, *The General Says No* (Harmondsworth: Penguin Books Ltd., 1963), pp. 43–5.
2. Roy Pryce, *The Politics of the European Community* (London: Butterworths, 1973), pp. 4–5.
3. Robert Lieber, *British Politics and European Unity* (Berkeley and Los Angeles: University of California Press, 1970), p. 23.
4. Ibid., p. 24.

5. Pryce, op. cit., chapter 1 for historical review on the development of Community institutions.
6. Lieber, op. cit., p. 21.
7. Ibid., pp. 31–2.
8. Ibid., pp. 32–3; Waltz, op cit., p. 232.
9. Lieber, pp. 33–5; Waltz, p. 233.
10. Lieber, pp. 73–4.
11. Waltz, op. cit., pp. 235–6.
12. Beloff, op. cit., p. 113.
13. Ibid., pp. 143ff.
14. Ibid., pp. 162ff.
15. Ibid., chapter 12 reviews the factors which appeared to play at least some role in de Gaulle's decision.
16. Miriam Camps, *European Unification in the Sixties* (New York: McGraw-Hill Co., 1966), pp. 157–60.
17. Ibid., p. 158.
18. Ibid., pp. 161ff.
19. Ibid., p. 165.
20. Ibid., pp. 163ff.; Lieber, op. cit., pp. 244–5.
21. Camps, op. cit., p. 171.
22. Ibid., p. 176.
23. Lieber, op. cit., p. 247.
24. Pryce, op. cit., pp. 20–1.
25. Ibid., p. 25; Robert J. Lieber, *Oil and the Middle East War: Europe in the Energy Crisis* (Cambridge, Mass.: Harvard Studies in International Affairs, No. 35, 1976), p. 20.
26. Pryce, pp. 103–4.
27. Concerning energy policy in the Community, and recent British unwillingness to go along with a collective policy, see *The Economist* (8 November 1975), p. 42; 13 December 1975, p. 40. On the aftermath of the referendum, see for example *The Economist* (5 June 1976), p. 55.
28. Pryce, op. cit., pp. 172–3.
29. William and Helyn Wallace, "The Impact of Community Membership on the British Machinery of Government", *Journal of Common Market Studies*, vol. xi, no. 4 (June 1973), pp. 243–62. There are indications that the Committee of Permanent Representatives, made up of members' ambassadors to the Community and their deputies, is an effective decision-making body despite lack of visibility. Foreign Secretary David Owen has encouraged strengthening it; see *The Economist* (2 July 1977), p. 14.

Chapter 5

1. Epstein, op. cit., p. 13.
2. Herbert Nicholas, *Britain and the U.S.A.* (Baltimore: Johns Hopkins Press, 1963), p. 22; Fox, op. cit., p. 27.
3. Samuel Flagg Bemis, *A Diplomatic History of the United States* (New York: Holt, Rinehart and Winston Inc., 1965), pp. 204–5, 252–3.
4. Ibid., pp. 407ff; Bruce Russett, *Community and Contention—Britain and*

America in the Twentieth Century (Cambridge, Mass.: MIT Press, 1963), p. 1.
5. Bagehot, op. cit., especially chapter 6.
6. Russett, op. cit., pp. 2ff.
7. Ibid., pp. 4–7.
8. Bemis, op. cit., p. 594.
9. Ibid., pp. 700ff.; Gore-Booth, op. cit., p. 227.
10. Pierre, op. cit., p. 47.
11. Nicholas, op. cit., pp. 60ff.
12. Ibid., pp. 65–6.
13. Bemis, op. cit., pp. 982–3.
14. Neustadt, op. cit., provides one of the most specifically detailed and comprehensive analyses available on the Skybolt crisis.
15. Arthur Schlesinger Jr. in *A Thousand Days* (Boston: Houghton Mifflin Co., 1965), chapter 32, is interesting for the sympathetic, but none-theless informative, treatment of the dilemmas facing Atlantic policy during the Kennedy years.
16. Schlesinger, op. cit., pp. 858ff.
17. Neustadt, op. cit., pp. 47–8.
18. As an example, cf. Wilson's uncertainty about whether Vietnam would cloud a forthcoming meeting with President Johnson in 1966—Wilson, op. cit., pp. 341–2.
19. On differences over the Middle East war, see for example Z, "The Year of Europe?" *Foreign Affairs* (January 1974), pp. 237–48.
20. On the British role in the test-ban treaty, see for instance, Schlesinger, op. cit., pp. 376–7, 893ff.
21. Nicholas, op. cit., pp. 172–3.

Chapter 6

1. Waltz, op. cit., p. 265.
2. Hoffmann, op. cit., p. 443.
3. Northedge, op. cit., p. 8; Vital, op. cit., p. 22.
4. Fox, op. cit., p. 12.
5. Samuel Beer, "The Future of British Politics: An American View", *Political Quarterly*, Vol. XXVI (January/March 1955), pp. 33–42.
6. Charles Lindblom's principal work on this theme is *The Intelligence of Democracy: Decision-Making Through Mutual Adjustment* (New York: The Free Press, 1965).
7. David Braybrooke and Charles Lindblom, *A Strategy of Decision* (New York: The Free Press, 1963), pp. 71ff.

Index